# How to Write a Book!

## To Get More Opportunities and Improve Your Career

*For Cynthia,*
*Another Book for*
*Your Bookshelf!*

*Andreas*

## Andreas Ramos

**andreas.com**

## Dedication

For Ronda & Michelle

# Table of Contents

# About this Book

## *Why this Book?*

Many of my friends and colleagues say the same thing: they want to write a book. They said I should write a book for them on how to write books.

This book is for my friends. This book tells you why you should write a nonfiction book to advance your career and build your credibility.

This isn't a "bestseller in a weekend" or "write a book in 21 days." The point isn't to bang out a book as fast as a monkey can type. That type of book won't help your reputation.

The point is for you to write something worthwhile and useful. People will respect your knowledge and tell others about you. This will help your career.

This isn't a guide to writing or a guide to self publishing. There are excellent books for that. Here are my notes on why I write books and how it works for me. I hope this will be useful for you.

## *The Audience for this Book*

To have the experience and background to write useful books, you should be mid-level or higher in your field with at least 3-5 years of experience. That gives you the 10,000 hours of experience to be an expert that Malcolm Gladwell writes about in *Blink*.

This book is a guide for writing nonfiction books, such as books for business, education, tech, and how-to.

Some of this can also be used for fiction. Fiction writing is different in some ways, but the work of writing and publishing is the same.

## My Experience in Writing

Here's what I've done as a writer:

- **Published Books:** This is my tenth book. My last three books were published by McGraw-Hill in the United States and Tsinghua University Press in Beijing (Tsinghua is the MIT of China). Another three books were published by Jain Press, an academic publisher. My books have been published in Denmark, Sweden, Finland, Germany, France, the UK, Spain, the United States, Mexico, China, and Taiwan.

- **Technical Writer:** I've done technical writing since the late 80s. I've written quite a few manuals for a wide range of companies, so it's likely you've read one of my manuals.

- **Technical Publications:** Starting in the mid-90s, I became a tech pubs manager, which means I was the editor and manager of technical publications. I produced 20-30 computer manuals at SUN, SGI, and other companies. In addition to writing manuals, I also managed teams of writers, editors, and illustrators.

- **Trade Group:** For ten years, I was the national chairman of the National Writers Union (NWU), a trade union affiliated with the UAW. It's the union for technical writers and business writers.

- My articles have been published in magazines and an additional twenty-one books, including US high school history books and university text books.

Overall, I've been in writing since the mid-80s as a writer, editor, publisher, and union organizer. Dozens of friends are professional writers.

## The Book's Advisors

The following people read drafts of the manuscript and contributed many ideas. They include: Alok Vasudeva (Sunnyvale), Alston Ghafourifar (Palo Alto), Brienne Ghafourifar (Palo Alto), Camilo Villa (Bogota), Carla King (San Diego), Fred Ramos (Palo Alto), Helen Gong (Palo Alto), Ken Chang (Shanghai), Lisa Carlson (Oakland), Mike Moran (New Jersey), Patti Wilson (Santa Cruz), Raul Ramos y Sanchez (Ohio), Renee Ramos (Palo Alto), Roslyn Layton (Copenhagen), Suzana Gorea (Paris), Vo Walle (San Jose), and Wendy Chang (San Francisco).

## The Chapter on Copyediting

Chapter 6, "Working with Copyeditors," was written by Lisa Carlson for this book. Hilary Powers participated in reviewing and editing the chapter.

## The Interviews

Publishing is evolving rapidly. To get a view of publishing from all sides, I talked with publishers and authors. Their comments and ideas had a significant impact on this book.

I interviewed the following authors and publishers. Most of them have published several books. The interviews are in the book and the book's webpage:

- Bruce Hartford, Civil rights, San Francisco
- Carla King, Motorcycle books, San Diego
- David Smith, Business books, Silicon Valley
- Dawn Wynne, Children's books, Los Angeles
- Eva Maria Knudsen, Parenting books, Denmark
- Gillian Bagwell, Historical fiction, Berkeley
- Mike Moran, Computer books, New Jersey
- Mukesh Jain, Publisher, Jain Publishing

- Raul Ramos y Sanchez, Fiction novelist, Ohio

- Roger Stewart, Acquisitions Editor, McGraw-Hill Education

- Susan Levitt, Astrology, San Francisco

## Illustration, Editing, and Production

A team of people helped in producing this book:

- Copyediting arranged by Lisa Carlson at UC Berkeley Extension. Copyeditors included: Gillian Bagwell (team leader) (GillianBagwell@hotmail.com), Isabelle Pouliot (Isabelle@desiu.ca), Jennifer Skancke (jen.skancke@gmail.com), Lori Spitz, Sean Morales (SeanFMorales@gmail.com), Steven Nelson (SroyNelson@gmail.com)

- Cover by Ginger Namgostar of SayItGraphicDesign.com, Sacramento

- Layout by Anaximander Katzenjammer, Palo Alto

## This Book's Resources Page: Updates and Downloads

For updates and free material, go to this book's webpage at Andreas.com.

## About the Author

I've lived and worked in Silicon Valley since 1995. I'm the Manager of Global SEO at Cisco. I'm also a professor of marketing at the Silicon Valley Business School. I'm on the advisory board of Entefy, ShanghaiValley.com, the Silicon Valley Red Cross, ClassJunky, EzyInsights, and several other Silicon Valley startups.

I was a technical publications manager at SGI, SUN, NTT, and over 20 dotcom startups, where I wrote and produced more than 75 printed computer manuals. I co-founded two digital marketing agencies. The second one got investor funding, opened offices in Palo Alto and Bangalore and grew to 175 employees. I was a director of digital marketing at Acxiom.

I've spoken at conferences, including New York City, Chicago, San Francisco, Los Angeles, Beijing, Shanghai, Aarhus, Mexico City, Paris, and Vienna.

As my pro bono work, I manage the worldwide Google AdWords campaign for MIT's Opencourseware Project (OCW), which is funded by a US$1m Google Foundation Grant. I do this because education enables people to lead better lives, improve the world, and end conflict.

I live with my wife and cat in Palo Alto. Visit me at Andreas.com.

# 1. Why Write a Book?

## Introduction

So why write a book? Quite simply: A book brings you opportunities. You'll be offered speaking engagements, projects, jobs, dates, invitations to join advisory boards, and invitations to start companies.

Why do books matter so much? Because people know from their own experience that it's really hard to write a book. It's hard to get the motivation or find the time. The process is complex and mostly unexplained.

This gives you an advantage. The Pareto Rule shows that in any field, about 20% of the participants get 80% of the revenues. Why? When people want help, they could research, investigate, compare, and do many things to solve their problem. Or they take a shortcut and go to the top experts. That's why the top people get most of the business and revenues in their field.

The more opportunities you have, the greater your security. Patti Wilson, a leading Silicon Valley job counselor, says, "Job security is the ability to get another job."

It's not about making money with books. As you'll see, most writers don't earn much from their books. But writing brings you get opportunities, which lead to revenues.

## One Book... or Six Books?

Throughout the 1990s and 2000s, I wrote a book every few years. Each book was a stand-alone project: I wrote the book, made a website for it, did marketing for it, but there was no connection between the books.

How to Write a Book! by Andreas Ramos

That changed when I wrote a book about content marketing. As I began to look at the role of books, I realized I had to write books not as separate projects, but as parts of a larger project. I also realized I should be writing a book every year, which is what I'll do from now on. In 2013, I released *The Big Book of Content Marketing* in March, *#TwitterBook* (a book about Twitter) in October, and the *SEO eBook* in December. For 2014, I wrote this book on how to write books. I'm researching for a book on influencers, to be published in 2015.

Books are also a social activity: you deal with many people as you write your book. You interview experts, talk with other writers, and meet people in companies. You work with developmental editors, copyeditors, subject matter experts, and illustrators. You're interviewed by magazines, radio, and TV. You speak at bookstore events, tradeshows, and conferences. You'll also meet and talk with quite a few of your readers. All of this brings you connections.

When you write a second book, those meetings also happen. Your connections start to rapidly expand. The more you write, the more people you'll meet.

So stop thinking about that one book you'll write. Start thinking you'll write six books!

You're wondering where you'll get so much material for six books. Don't worry. You'll see how to do that in this book.

## Should You Go for Quantity or Quality?

Okay, so can you write just anything? Does quality matter?

Yes, it has to be really good. Why? Because good stuff goes far. The higher the quality, the less you'll need to promote your book. People seek out the best work. People share great information with their friends. Nobody shares just-okay stuff. So write good books. In this book, I'll also show you how to do that.

## Why Will Anyone Listen to You?

Several have asked me, "But I'm not an expert! Why will anyone listen to me?"

If you have a bit of experience in your field and do a bit of research, you'll be ahead of most of your colleagues. They want your experience and knowledge. You don't have to be #1. Just be ahead of many others.

## Writing Nonfiction vs. Fiction Books

One of the differences between nonfiction and fiction is the purpose of the book. Nonfiction is written by people who are experts in their field and the book is to be read by others in the same field.

Fiction, on the other hand, rarely requires expertise in the topic. No science fiction author has spent time on another planet. There may be research, but it's not based on years of hands-on experience. The audience for fiction can be just about anyone, not only specialists.

Nonfiction authors write books as part of their profession. They write to educate others and to further their careers. Nonfiction books may sell only a few thousand copies, but that's okay; the authors earn their living from their profession. Their books attract clients and projects, which result in income. It's not the books, it's the clients who matter.

Fiction writers are either so successful with best sellers that they can live from their book income, or if their books aren't best sellers, they have jobs or spouses. People who write detective novels aren't working detectives. In fact, the reality of detective work (or any profession) is too boring for fiction. A fiction writer earns only a few dollars per book, so she must sell 30-50,000 copies per year. In contrast, the nonfiction writer can be successful with only a few thousand books because she doesn't depend on book sales for her income.

The shelf life of the book is another difference between nonfiction and fiction. *Moby Dick*, written in 1851, is still read today. But it's safe to say that no manual on whaling from even twenty years ago is read today.

Technology and processes change so rapidly now that nonfiction books are often useless after a few years.

Finally, another difference between fiction and nonfiction writers is their social activity. Fiction writers tend to write alone. A few friends may review the manuscript, but in general, the book is the product of the writer's mind. James Salter points out the writing of poetry is entirely solitary. In nonfiction writing, the author collaborates with many people. The manuscript is read by people who are familiar with the topic. The publisher will assign project managers, developmental editors, copyeditors, and others to improve the text. Several dozen people can be involved in the writing and editing of a nonfiction book. This brings the writer in closer working contact with his field.

## The Relationship between Authors and Readers

Let's look at the relation between writers and their audience. In any social community (such as writing, music, medicine, telecoms, etc.), there are three kinds of participants: the creators who create new ideas, the commenters who talk about those ideas, and the audience.

- **Creators:** 1% of the community is creators. Creators create new ideas, set the agenda, and lead the field. They're the influencers. Your goal is to become a creator in your field. You do this by creating authoritative content, offering leadership by advocacy, and setting an agenda.

- **Commenters:** 9% of the community is comprised of commenters. The commenters discuss the work of the creative 1%: they're critics, reviewers, editorialists, pundits, bloggers, and so on. They could be staff of a publication or self-appointed with a blog. You should encourage critics to comment on your books, but they're not your audience.

- **Audience:** 90% of the people in your community are your audience. The audience follows both creators and commenters. They buy and read books. They also share your books with their friends and co-workers. Encourage your audience to comment, rate, vote, review, distribute, and share your content.

If you become part of the 1%, commenters will discuss what you write. The 90% will read about it. This means you can reach 99% of your audience.

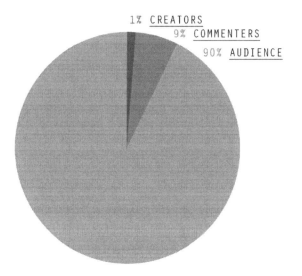

Figure 1: The 90/9/1 Rule: Any social activity is made up of creators (1%), commenters (9%), and followers (90%). By being in the 1%, you can reach 99%.

For example, the world of music is made up of musicians, critics, and fans. The musicians, who are the 1%, write songs and perform music. The critics, who are 9%, write about the performers and their music. The fans make up 90% of the music community. They listen to bands, buy music, and go to concerts.

This behavior of participants in communities has been extensively studied in sociology. I wrote about this in my book *The Big Book of Content Marketing*.

## Your Role as an Author: Be a Thought Leader

The 1% set the field's agenda, define the topics that are discussed, and drive the future of the field. You should be a creator and be in the 1%:

- Carry out original research. What information is needed? What's missing? You have experience and you know about your field, so see what's lacking and write about it.

- Offer advocacy and leadership. Don't just participate in your field. Take a clear position and tell others. What should your field do? Push the field forward.

- Speak at conferences, write articles, and publish books.

- Look at the ideas that everyone holds as true in your field. Does it really work that way? Or is it a sacred cow? Are people doing things just because everyone else does it?

You can see this can't be assigned to a staffer, a PR person, or a marketing agency. They don't have your experience and knowledge.

## Your Role as a Commenter

Along with being a creator, you can also look at books by others and offer your comments on why something is useful or why it's wrong. This helps your audience see the big picture.

However, your focus should be on creating new content, not presenting the work of others. Commenting shouldn't be mindless collecting. Lazy writers create lists of "12 Secrets, 6 Tips, and 3 Basics." Anyone can spend ten minutes in a search engine, collect links, and send that out. Don't do stuff like that. You should select useful items and add your comments. When you tell people why something is important, you guide them.

You can also comment on your own whitepapers, FAQs, or PowerPoints. Add short summaries and explain why they're useful. Post this monthly or quarterly to your blog and distribute it by email.

## Is this Really 90/9/1?

I see a hand raised with a question. Someone is asking if the breakdown of creators, commenters, and audience is precisely 90/9/1. Sociologists studied many kinds of groups and found the ratios depend on the group:

- Professor Akil Awan at the University of London examined jihad forums in 2005 and found 87% of the audience never posted to the forums; 13% posted at least once; 5% posted 50 times or more; and 1% posted 500 times or more

- On Wikipedia, 50% of edits are made by 2.5% of users

- Wildfire looked at 10,000 Facebook campaigns over nine months and found 83% of users were passive viewers, 15.4% were commenters, and 1.5% were creators

- Every one of IBM's 433,000 employees has their own employee webpage, which includes a blog. About 6% of them (26,000 employees) post to their blog. 1.2% (5,200) of IBM employees post five times or more.

In general, the ratio ranges from 0.5% to 2.5% for creators, 10% to 15% for commenters, and 85% to 90% for the passive audience.

## Your Partner

Okay, here's the first insider tip about writing. Writing takes a lot of time, so your partner or spouse should be supportive. He or she should understand why you're doing this and make allowances for the time you put into it. Books are good for both of you: they improve your opportunities, career, security, and income. That's why books are often dedicated to significant others; they make it possible for you to write.

## Summary of this Chapter

You write nonfiction books to build your career. Because only 1% of the people in a field are the leaders, you'll be seen as a leader. You'll be offered projects, jobs, and opportunities.

　　　　　　　　　　How to Write a Book! by Andreas Ramos

# 2. Calendar, Team, Research

## Introduction

Let's look at how to create a project calendar, build your writing team, and research your topic.

## Three Phases in a 90-Day Writing Calendar

The popular conception of writing has someone write in solitary for years until they finish a long manuscript. That's Hollywood. Reality is quite different.

There are three phases to writing your book. You research to write an outline, fill out the outline to make a first draft, which you polish to make a final draft.

Convert these three phases into a 90-day writing calendar:

| Month | Phase | Action |
|-------|-------|--------|
| **First Month** | Research and Outline | Research your topic, make notes, jot down ideas, brainstorm, and conduct interviews. |
| **Second Month** | First Draft | Organize your notes into an outline. Send the outline for review. Fill out the outline. The result is your first draft. Send the first draft to your developmental editor and subject matter experts for their comments and feedback. |
| **Third Month** | Second Draft | Clean up and rewrite each section to turn the first draft into your final draft. Send the final draft to copyeditors who fix the grammar, spelling, and style. |

The sequence is important. Don't edit before you finish the first draft. Otherwise, you'll get tied up in editing and you won't finish the draft.

The same for the final draft: finish it before you send it to copyeditors. The copyeditors should see a manuscript that's ready for layout. Otherwise, if you make changes after they edit, you'll add new errors.

## The Three-Phase Process vs. the Usual Way of Writing

Many non-professional writers write a long manuscript. They'll add, write, edit, and research pretty all at the same time. They'll write a chapter, edit it, and then write another chapter. This can go on for several years. I've met people who've been working on their book for three years or more. When they finally finish, they give copies of the manuscript to others for comments. The book's general structure has already been set, so the comments are generally minor edits or a few suggestions. The book is the product of a solitary author.

In contrast, professional non-fiction writers work in teams. The outline is sent to the developmental editor and subject matter experts (perhaps two dozen people) who make structural suggestions to the outline and add or delete chapters or sections. Feedback happens before the first draft is started. By adding the knowledge and experience of a large group of professionals, the book becomes richer. The book is the product of a team instead of a solitary writer. The 90-day calendar and the deadlines also force the team to focus their attention.

## What If You Have Changes after the Deadline?

You must use deadlines. If you don't, it will never end. There's always more to be added and changes to be made. Set the deadlines on the first day of your project.

If you're writing for a publisher, the deadline is serious. The publisher has a large team of people who are working on a production calendar. If you take your book off the production schedule, use a few weeks to make changes, and then try to get in again, there may be no space in the production calendar for you. They've moved on to the next book.

How to Write a Book! by Andreas Ramos

# Build Your Writing Team

While you're researching, you can also put together your writing team:

| Title | Job Description |
|-------|-----------------|
| Author | The author of nonfictions books has several years of experience and a working knowledge of the field. |
| Acquisitions Editor | The acquisitions editor acquires the books at the publishing house. He knows the market, looks for new writers, and works with previously-published writers. He reads proposals, selects manuscripts, and turns them over to the project manager. |
| Project Manager (PM) | The project manager (PM) manages the book production process. She identifies the roles, assigns people to the roles, sets up the calendar, supervises the deliveries, makes sure everyone is in step, and sets the deadlines. |
| Developmental Editor | The developmental editor plans the organization of the content, selects categories and formats, edits headings and outlines, rewrites, restructures content, deletes content to improve flow, and identifies gaps in content. He should be familiar with your field. |
| Subject Matter Experts (SME) | Subject Matter Experts (SME) are people with experience and knowledge of your subject. They review the first draft and make suggestions and changes. These can include colleagues and co-workers. You can also include a few non-experts to make sure your book is clear to everyone. You should have about 20 subject matter experts. |
| Copyeditor | The copyeditor checks voice, clarity, spelling, grammar, punctuation, capitalization, list numbering, illustration labeling, subject-verb agreement, and consistency. She removes wordiness, triteness, convoluted text, and jargon. She checks the content against the style manual. Copyeditors are critical for producing quality. Copyeditor is one word. |
| Layout Editor | The layout editor is an expert with fonts, line spacing, and page layout. She also adjusts headings, footers, and pagination. She's the one who turns text into a book. |
| Brand Editor | The brand editors ensures the text and illustrations comply with the company's brand guidelines. |
| Proofreader | The proofreader checks the final text against the layout to make sure that all of the changes were made. He also checks pagination, line breaks, and captions. |

When you read books by authors published by big publishers, you think, Wow, that writer writes so well! No, that's the team: the writer, the developmental editor, subject matter experts, and copyeditors. They took a good text and turned it into professional writing.

The writer is part of a team. This is like the movies, where Tom Cruise gets the credit but the movie is the work of dozens of people. My books generally include two to three dozen people.

Authors who work in fiction often belong to writing groups, where a circle of authors share their manuscripts for group review. You can use the web or your local library to find writing groups in your city.

## Co-Authors for Your Book

You can also write a book with co-authors. If someone gets their name on the cover, then they should participate substantially in the project management.

You also need to decide how to share the royalties with your co-author. It can be an even split, 60/40, 82/18 or whatever both of you agree on. This may also require tracking of revenues for several years, which can become quite a bit of extra work.

In my experience, it's best not to have co-authors. If your co-author doesn't deliver on time, you'll write his part. This can lead to awkward discussions about the co-author's name on the cover and royalties.

You can invite people to write chapters or sections in your book and list them as contributors in the preface.

## What Should You Write About?

Your goal is to become known as an expert in your field. You should develop a series of books that cover each of the areas in your field. Start by looking at the overview of your field and make a list of the various areas. This also forces you to learn your field. You don't need to have a conclusive list before you start. As you learn more about your field, you'll discover new areas for topics. Think about a five- or six-year campaign to write books for each topic.

## Must You Be an Expert Before You Start Writing?

Of course not! Politicians write lots of books and they don't have any idea of what they're saying.

Don't worry. Because you have experience and you did research (wait, you did the research, didn't you?), you'll be an expert.

## Research for Your Book

In the research phase, learn as much as you can about your subject. Talk with people, read books and articles, and think about the topic:

- Go to a research library, look up your topic, and see what you can learn.

- You can also look at college textbooks.

- Go to major bookstores and Amazon to buy the leading books on your topic. I generally buy 15-25 books for each book I write.

- Use the web. Read about your topic in Wikipedia. Look at blogs, articles, white papers, PDFs, and so on.

- Interview people who have experience and knowledge of your topic. Meet them for coffee or lunch. Ask a few general questions and let them talk. They'll point out many things that you didn't think about.

- Many ideas will occur to you when you're walking the dog. Write them down immediately or you'll forget.

Don't worry about organization or direction at this point. Write down everything. It's much better to have too many ideas than too few.

Carry a notepad with you all the time so you can jot down ideas. You can use Evernote or Google Docs on your cell phone. You can also send text messages to yourself. Use whatever works for you.

You'll end up with a squirrel's nest of ideas and notes on napkins, receipts, the back of uncancelled checks, sticky notes, emails, and SMS messages. Collect all of this in one file with an item on each line.

## Research Your Audience and their Interests

What does your audience really want to know? What are your audience's problems? What are their motivations? There are several ways to do this:

- Look at question-and-answer sites where people ask questions and others answer. Questions are sorted by categories, so you can see what people are thinking about. Sites include Yahoo! Answers (answers.yahoo.com), AllExperts, theanswerbank.co.uk, and Quora.

- Search in Twitter. You can search for keywords or hashtags. Scroll back six months, copy all of the postings, and review those.

- Collect questions from your sales and support team. They know customers' "top ten common questions."

- Put a prominent "Ask us a question" box at your website and collect the questions.

- Look at your own blog. Look at your readers' comments to see what they find interesting.

- Look at your website's search box. If configured correctly, your web analytics can give you a list of queries.

For example, when I was writing the book on content marketing, I searched for "content marketing" at a large question-and-answer site and found 384 questions. 41 questions were useful for the book.

Figure 2: You can use Wordle to see a word cloud of the discussion among computer network administrators. These combine the conversation, find the most frequent words, and create a visual display to show you what the community is talking about. In this example, you can see that security and malware are significant topics.

You can also create word clouds of blogs. Here's my blog:

Figure 3: You can create a word cloud of someone's blog or tweets to see what they write about.

## How to Make a Tweet Cloud

You can make a tweet cloud in a few steps (it's easy):

- Go to a person's tweets and scroll down to six months of tweets or a few hundred tweets

- Click at the end, hold down Shift, go to the top, click to select all, and copy the tweets

- Paste the tweets in a text editor such as Notepad.

- Go to Wordle.net, click Create, and paste the tweets

- Wordle turns the tweets into a word cloud. However, some words will be large because they're repeated often, such as the person's name, his Twitter ID, or the names of months. Go back to the text editor and use Search/Replace All to get rid of those. Copy the result and post it to Wordle again. Repeat this a few times until you get a useful result.

## How Do I Get Funding to Write a Book?

There are several ways to fund your book project:

- You pay your own bills. Either you have savings or you have a job so you write at night and weekends.

- The publisher gives you an advance. If you have a large publisher, you may be offered an advance on the royalties based on expected sales. Generally, you get half on signing the contract and the second half when you deliver the manuscript.

- If you write for someone, the client pays you. You can be paid on salary, by the hour, or by the project.

- There is also crowdfunding.

## Can I Get Crowdfunding for My Book?

Crowdfunding has become a popular way to support music bands, theater productions, and indie movies. It's also possible to use crowdfunding to support a writing project. Writers propose ideas, set funding goals, and people donate funds. Authors have raised anywhere from US$10,000 to $40,000 for their projects.

You can offer various things to contributors: they can be listed on the thank-you page, they can appear as characters in your book, or you can send them an autographed book or the T-shirt of the book.

How to Write a Book! by Andreas Ramos

There are crowdfunding sites for writers, such as Inkshare, Pubslush, and Unbound.com (UK). You can also look into crowdfunding sites such as Kickstarter or Indiegogo.

## Summary of this Chapter

To prepare your project, set a calendar, build a team, and research your topic. The next step is the outline.

# The Author Speaks: Raul Ramos y Sanchez

Raul Ramos y Sanchez is an award-winning author of the Class H Trilogy of novels which include *America Libre, House Divided*, and *Pancho Land*. He began the series in 2003 with the input of scholars from the U.S., Latin America, and Spain. The series was published by Grand Central Publishing and Beck & Branch Publishing. Visit him at RaulRamos.com. (Raul and Andreas aren't related! Ed. Note.)

## Why Do You Write?

Because I can't afford to produce my own movies. A book, I can finish on my own.

## How Has Writing Affected Your Life and Career?

The research, execution, and promotion of my novels has taken me to places and introduced me to people I'd never have otherwise encountered. It's the single most satisfying aspect of my professional career, most of which has been spent in marketing.

## Do You Prefer Self Publishing or Traditional?

My first two novels were published by Grand Central Publishing. On the advice of my agent, we published the third independently through Beck & Branch Publishing. An excellent incentive of self publishing is the superior profit on each book. The downside is that many in the media still look down on self-published books, which makes it harder to promote these books.

## What Are Your Experiences with Self Publishing?

What I like about indie publishing: More creative freedom for the author in title, cover, and other promotional options. The author can sell fewer books to make the same amount of money with print-on-demand and e-books. What I don't like about indie publishing: it's glutted with poorly-written and poorly-edited books. As a result, an indie author must overcome the perception of being second rate.

## What's Your Experience with Traditional Publishing?

Traditional publishers usually have superb editors. Not only will your manuscript be thoroughly proofed and indexed, you'll also get very sound advice on improving the narrative. At the same time, traditional publishers can be high-handed and dismissive. A new author's opinion on the promotional material is rarely welcomed.

## Do You Have an Agent?

My agent has been a valuable ally as well as the person with the contacts at major publishers. An agent also adds a degree of credibility if you choose the indie route. Of course that means sharing your profits.

## Did a Lawyer Review Your Contract?

I didn't use a lawyer to review my publishing contract since my agent had arranged many similar deals.

## What's the Best Way to Promote Your Book?

If I knew the answer to that, I'd be selling a lot more books. The conclusion I've come to after many years in the publishing world is to write the very best book you can. At worst, you'll have something to be proud of.

## What Would You Have Done Differently?

Started earlier. Every writer I know feels their last book was their best.

# 3. Writing the Outline

To make an outline, you sort and organize your research notes into a logical structure. The outline is most of the work in your project. If you have a good outline, the text is easy to write. If you have a weak outline (or no outline), your text will be a shallow mess. Nearly every writer that I talked with agreed on this: The outline is critical to writing a book.

## *Turn Your Research Notes into an Outline*

There are several ways to write outlines. You can use 6x4 index cards. Put a heading at the top and add notes on the rest of the card. Cards are easy to arrange (and rearrange) on a table or the floor until you have your outline. You can also use Microsoft Word, Adobe Framemaker, or Scrivener.

Let's say your research resulted in six hundred notes. Here's how to use these notes to write an outline in Microsoft Word:

- When you've finished your research, collect all of your six hundred notes into one file. I put everything into one document in Word. Don't worry about order. Just put it all in a Word file.

- Give each note a short heading. At this point, the heading's text is just for you, so just say exactly what it is. Go through all six hundred notes and give them descriptive headings. Be sure to use an H3 style for the headings.

- In Word, switch to Outline view. This shows your text as an outline. In Word 2010, select View | Outline. This opens Outlining, a new tab. Click Outlining to see tools for Outline view. Click on Show Level and select Level 2 or Level 3 (depending on how you set up the format styles for your headings). This converts your manuscript into an outline view so you'll see only headings.

- Look at the heading of the first note. What chapter should it be in? Type a chapter heading and set the chapter heading to Level 1. For example, is it a note about writing, publishing, or selling? If it's a note about selling, create a chapter heading called Selling and move the note to that chapter.

- Look at the second note. Does it fall into the same category as the first? If yes, leave it under that category. If not, give it a new category heading.

- Look at the third note. Do the same as before. Either move it into a chapter or create a new chapter for it. If the note is about publishing, then create a chapter called Publishing.

- At this point, don't organize the notes within the chapters. The goal here is to sort the six hundred notes into chapters. Just drag and drop.

- The next step is to organize the notes within a chapter. Move the notes around until they match the work flow of what you're trying to describe. You'll soon start to notice missing steps, so write notes for those. You'll also see several notes say the same thing. You can either combine them or delete the extras. You'll end up with long chapters with many notes.

- See if chapters can break into smaller chapters. For example, my chapter on Writing had several topics: General Comments about Writing, Tools for Writing, Legal Stuff about Writing, More Stuff about Writing, and so on. (See? I use plain words for chapters. Easier to understand.)

Your outline will evolve. Start with an outline, but don't feel obligated to keep it as it is. As you learn more about your topic, you'll realize that some parts will make better sense if they're combined, separated, or moved. The outlining tool lets you quickly restructure your manuscript. As you make changes, the manuscript is automatically updated.

How to Write a Book! by Andreas Ramos

You'll also have a collection of ideas and notes that don't fit into the book. No problem. Put those in another file. Maybe you can use them for your next book.

Take your time on the outline. I may spend a week or more on the outline. The better the outline, the easier to write the text.

### Get a Review of Your Outline

When you've finished the outline, show it to your developmental editor, your subject matter experts, and your publisher. They can suggest additions, deletions, changes, and improvements. This ensures you didn't forget something. Often, they can suggest a better way to structure your thoughts.

### Why an Outline?

Why does an outline make it easier to write? The outline is the structure of your book and your thoughts. After you have a good outline, you can write quickly because all you have to do is write a paragraph to explain each item in the outline.

For example, in the chapter *Legal Stuff about Writing,* I added the notes about copyright and contracts. I noticed people also asked about plagiary, pirates, and legal permissions, so I added more notes. I then put the list into a logical order and filled out each item. That chapter was written in two days.

### Your Outline and Vegetable Gardens

Let's illustrate this with an example. Let's say you want to turn your backyard into a vegetable garden. You could go out there one day and plant some tomatoes here, some garlic over there, and some corn as well. But you'll end up with a mess of a garden with stuff growing all over the place.

The way to plant a garden is to first sit down at the kitchen table, make a list of the stuff you like to eat, and then on a piece of paper, make an drawing of where the plants will go in your garden. You can also make it look good by putting the low plants in front and tall plants at the back with sunflowers. Finally, with the plan in your hand, you buy the seeds and plant your garden.

See? The planting part is just filling out the plan. The same with books: the writing part is just filling out the outline.

This is why many people have problems with writing books. They just jump in and start writing lots of text with the hope that somehow it will turn into a book. That's like throwing a bag of seeds in your backyard and expecting a garden. The birds will be happy!

It's not really their fault. Endless Hollywood movies show an author who gets struck by inspiration or a brick and he sits down at a typewriter, knocks out a best seller, and gets the girl. I've been hit in the head by plenty of bricks but I didn't get a book out of it. Outlining would be a boring Hollywood movie. No gin, no girls, no guns, no *Sunset Boulevard*.

Unskilled writers also make the mistake of endless revisions, trying to make it perfect. Since they don't have a structure for the text, they write a first draft, second draft, third draft, forty-fifth draft....

## Alternatives to Outlines: Mind Maps

Another way to outline is to use mind maps. I've used this for several projects and it works well. Mind maps allow you a non-linear visualization of you project. You add topics and the topics lead to other topics.

## Summary of this Chapter

The outline is the frame of the book. It gives structure, shape, and purpose to your book. A solid outline makes it easy to write the first draft.

# The Author Speaks: David Smith

David Smith is an entrepreneur with more than 30 years' experience in the high-tech sector. David has founded numerous startups in Silicon Valley, Europe, and Asia in online marketplaces, online education, software, multimedia, and Internet publishing. A former Apple World Marketing Manager, David is the founder and chair of Tynax., a global patent and technology exchange; founder and president of Silicon Valley Business School; founder and director of Silicon Valley High School; and author of *Patents, Cloaks & Daggers* (daggers.co), *Dollar Value* (DollarValue.co), and *Zero-to-IPO* (Zero-to-IPO.com). David holds a BSc. (Hons.) Computer Science & Economics from the University of Leeds and a J.D. from Santa Clara University School of Law.

## Why Do You Write?

To share what I've learned with people who need to know.

## How Has Writing Affected Your Life and Career?

Opened some doors and created some opportunities. Seems to establish credibility with some people.

## Do You Prefer Self Publishing or Traditional?

I don't see any reason why anyone would go for traditional publishing these days. Self publishing seems to be the logical approach.

## Did You Start with Traditional or Self-Publishing?

I started talking to publishers and authors. I realized I didn't need a publisher so I just focused on writing and publishing the book myself. I created my own publishing company to publish my books.

## What's Your Experience with Self Publishing?

Some people are stuck in the old, pre-Internet era and believe a publisher adds credibility. Fortunately, these are a dying breed.

### What's Your Experience with Traditional Publishing?

Never tried it. When I heard the publisher relies on the author to do the publicity and marketing, I couldn't see the point of going with a publisher.

### Do You Have an Agent?

No agent. Never considered it.

### Did a Lawyer Review Your Contract?

I'm a lawyer. Saving legal fees by reviewing my own contracts may help me recover the costs of law school.

### What's the Best Way to Promote Your Book?

I've been somewhat passive about promoting. I create a website for each book and let customers find it. Selling via Amazon.com was effective. Selling via stores and university bookshops was a painful experience—they take your books, sell some, and then return shop-worn and damaged books. That's a complete waste of time and energy.

### What Would You Have Done Differently?

I would have put more effort into online marketing and promotion of my books.

# 4. Writing the First Draft

So you wrote the outline. Your developmental editor, your expert advisors, and your publisher signed off on it. You're ready to start writing.

The goal in this stage is to fill out your outline. Under each section heading, you have a few notes or key words. Look at the note and write two or three short paragraphs to explain it. If you can get it in one paragraph, that's fine. If it takes five or six paragraphs, you may consider if it should be two entries.

There's a nice thing about the outline method. It keeps you from getting bored. If you get stuck on a section, go to another section. You can come back later. At this stage, you only have to describe each section, which can usually be done in a few paragraphs, so you don't have to write long sections.

When you've filled out all of the sections, you've finished the first draft.

The point of the first draft is to state the main ideas and their supporting arguments and evidence. When carpenters build a house, they first build the frame and then the walls. After the house is finished, you add furniture and carpets. Your first draft should show the skeleton of your book so the reviewers can see what you mean.

Don't edit your first draft (which means, don't edit for sentence structure, grammar, or clarity). It's hard to not do this. If you start editing, you'll get caught up in that instead of filling out the entries. Leave edits for later.

## Share the First Draft with Your Team

When you finish the first draft, share it with your subject matter experts and developmental editor for review of the ideas and content. They shouldn't edit for grammar, style, or punctuation.

The developmental editor knows what you're talking about and has experience in your field. She reviews for overall information and balance to make deep strategic changes. This chapter is weak. That section needs to be expanded. This section should be dropped. These additional issues should be covered.

The subject matter experts (SMEs, pronounced "smee") read your manuscript as readers (not editors). Subject matter experts should have at least five years of hands-on experience in your field. They tell you what matters and better yet, what doesn't matter. This makes your book useful to others. Don't meet in an office. Meet for lunch or coffee. The less formal, the more open they'll be.

After the developmental editor and your subject matter experts return the first draft to you, you add, expand, or delete sections. You end up with a solid first draft, which is the foundation for your book. There's still a lot of lumber and nails lying around, but that's okay. You have the frame for the house.

You don't have to wait to finish the first draft. As you finish each chapter, you can send it to your team. This brings up your project management skills: as you're writing chapter five, you've sent out chapter four and you're getting questions about chapter three. You're also working with the illustrator and the website developer. As the author and leader, you coordinate the project. Everything comes together on the 90th day of your calendar when you release the book for publishing. Just like when you worked at Burger Clown and made burgers, fries, and drinks all at the same time while six customers were yelling for their orders.

I generally find twenty to thirty subject matter experts for a book. They're a mix of professionals and non-professionals. Be sure to get a few readers who know nothing about your field. They'll let you know whether your manuscript makes sense.

Why 20 or 30 subject matter experts? Because only three or five of them will read the manuscript closely. In my experience, most promise to read it, but they won't have time and they'll only make a few suggestions.

## How Many Pages?

How short can it be? How long is too long? You've probably heard Mark Twain's joke, "I didn't have time to write a short letter, so I wrote a long one instead." It's easy to just write a lot and force the reader to figure it out. Short books are better because they're less work for the reader.

Books with only 50 or 75 pages are too light. However, the more you write, the fewer readers you'll have. Few people will read 400 pages. 150 to 200 pages are the most that most people will read. That's also enough to explain most topics.

It also depends on the field. If you're writing how-to or business books, 150 pages is common. For academic writing, books are often 250-350 pages. At 400 pages or more, the printing costs start to rise.

A printed book with 150 pages has about 50,000 words. This book has 51,888 words. To find out how many words you've written, use Microsoft Word to count words. Select Review | Word Count.

## Grammar and Punctuation

You should also know basic grammar and punctuation, including how to use citation marks, the serial comma, and abbreviations. You should also cite books properly. The citation standard depends on your field. Don't expect the copyeditor to fix this for you. For a short summary of punctuation rules, see ThePunctuationGuide.com. More guides are at the Bay Area Editors' Forum (BAEF) at EditorsForum.org. You can also get *The Chicago Manual of Style* and read the chapter on punctuation.

## Common Mistakes in Writing

Several mistakes can lead to poor writing:

- Bad writing often happens when the text is unstructured. The author wrote lots of sentences without researching, organizing with an outline, or working with editors. It's very difficult to restructure such a text. It's easier to start over.

- The inspired book is also a problem. The writer has a great idea and starts writing. After 20-30 pages, he has worked out the idea and then he has to fill another 100 pages. So he adds all sorts of junk until he has 150 pages and he writes *The End*, by which he really means *Thank God, It's over!*

- Another problem is the attempt to publish forty blog postings as a book. A blog post is usually a short discussion of an idea, so when you read it by itself, that's okay. But when you read many blog postings together in a book, you end up with forty ideas in forty directions.

## Use XX, YY, and ZZ to Mark Your Editing Places

A tip: use XX, YY, and ZZ as bookmarks in your manuscript. You can also use TK (*to come*) or RW (*rewrite*). You can develop your own codes.

When I write down an idea, it may be just a few words to remind me, such as "ISBN." So I write "ISBN XX." Place these markers as you're writing. Later, I look for unfinished sections. I search for XX and it brings me to an unfinished section. When I finish the section, I delete the XX. I search for XX again and it brings me to the next unfinished place.

I add YY to mark items to check later, such as book titles or if a website is still working. When I'm cleaning up the final draft, I search for YY and fix those.

A few things have to be updated at the last moment. For example, the title of the book should also be in the page footer, so I mark that with ZZ. Examples of things to update at the last moment are the ISBN or AIN number, the copyright date, the release date, and version number.

## Ghostwriters

Okay, so you still want a book but you don't have time to write. No problem. Hire a ghostwriter. He writes the book and it's published under your name. The ghostwriter doesn't mind because he's paid for that. Many business books and most books by movie stars, musicians, athletes, and politicians are written by ghostwriters.

*Lean In* by Sheryl Sandberg, the COO of Facebook, was written by Nell Scovell. John F. Kennedy's Pulitzer Prize-winning book *Profiles in Courage* was written by Ted Sorenson. Raymond Benson was the ghostwriter for a Tom Clancy novel. *Faith of my Fathers* by John McCain was written by Mark Salter. *It Takes a Village* by Hillary Clinton was written by Barbara Feinman. *I am Jackie Chan* by Jackie Chan was by Jeff Yang. *Dreams of my Father* by Obama is by Bill Ayers. And finally, *Decision Point*, the autobiography of George W. Bush, was written by Christopher Michel.

Be careful with ghostwriters. It's like those movies where the parents are bugging the poor guy to get married and he comes home with a fake girlfriend. What happens at a conference when the CEO gives a talk that was written by a ghostwriter and someone asks a detailed question? Or the ghostwriter gets a better offer from your competitor? Or decides to go dance with the elephants in Bhutan for three months?

Ghostwriting can range from $3,000 to $10,000 per month. The more you pay, the better the result. And the better the ghostwriter, the more you'll pay.

If you're a celebrity, CEO of a large company, or a politician, your publisher may arrange the ghostwriter. In that case, the ghost gets a share of royalties, the advance, and movie rights. For major books, this can be $500,000 up to several million dollars.

The ghostwriter will do the research, which includes long interviews with you. You'll get the outline and drafts so you can add or delete.

A good account of how ghostwriting happens (and how it turned into a disaster) is Andrew O'Hagan's ghostwriting of Julian Assange's autobiography (*The London Review of Books*, March 6, 2014, at http://goo.gl/71P29m). Despite a million-dollar advance and several dozen publishing contracts in other countries, it was impossible to get Assange to review the drafts.

## Where to Find Ghostwriters

There are several ways to find ghostwriters:

- Talk with your publisher. They often work with ghostwriters.

- Book agents and public relations firms also often use ghostwriters

- Look at the leading trade journals for your industry. Contact the editors and journalists to see if they'll write for you.

- Look for authors of books in your field. The authors may be able to write for you or they may recommend ghostwriters.

- Additional places to find ghostwriters include BlogDash, Blogmutt, Business2Blogger.com, Contently, and eCopyWriters

- You can also hire technical writers. They're highly experienced in writing books.

## Summary of this Chapter

With the outline as a guide, the first draft is a quick fill-in-the-blanks. You write a few short sentences or paragraphs for each outline point. This will let your reviewers understand what you mean.

# The Author Speaks: Dawn Wynne

Dawn Wynne's children's books are Amazon Best Sellers. She's also an award-winning educator with more than 15 of years experience teaching students from kindergarten through high school, including special-needs students, English language learners, and at-risk youth. Her newest book, *Earth Remembers When*, has earned two children's book awards. *I Remember When* was an Indie Excellence Finalist. *Earth Remembers When* won a Readers' Choice Award and a Living Now Award. She's written two books and is working on the third as well as a second edition for her book. She has been writing all of her life, but started publishing over the past five years. Before that, she wrote Hollywood screenplays and short films. Visit her at DawnWynne.com.

## *Why Do You Write?*

Most of my books are written to educate young children. I write about what inspires me and then translate those ideas to young children.

## *How Has Writing Affected Your Life and Career?*

Writing is a wonderful way to connect with people. It has allowed me to teach children but with a more flexible schedule. It hasn't afforded me a lavish lifestyle, but a more rewarding, satisfying career.

## *Do You Prefer Self Publishing or Traditional?*

Self publishing. I have more control over the content and illustrations. Traditional publishing still requires the author to do the same marketing and promotional work. While the upfront costs are greater, I also receive a larger profit for each book.

## *Did You Start with Traditional or Self-Publishing?*

Started with self publishing and have continued. I don't have to wait to get approval for the books I want to write. I have a say with my illustrator. And I can write books on my own timeline.

### What's Your Experience with Self Publishing?

I have my books printed in China so there can be some confusion with printing terms or techniques. While the printing may be cheaper, samples and prototypes can be costly to ship and take a little more time. My printers have been very helpful through the design and printing process. The biggest negative with self publishing isn't being able to distribute with the major distributors (Ingram, Baker, and Taylor). For a children's author this is key to get books into schools and libraries.

### What's the Best Way to Promote Your Book?

In-person appearances. When people see you and your book, they become interested and excited. Seeing a book in person brings it to life. It's hard to get people to buy your book just by seeing it online. When it comes to children's books, parents and children want to see the pictures. Reviews are helpful and add credibility.

### What Would You Have Done Differently?

I'd have cut my costs as much as possible so I could afford distribution services that would have allowed my books to reach a wider audience.

# 5. Writing the Final Draft

You now rewrite the first draft into the second draft, which is also called the final draft. You clean up sentences and create a final, polished text.

You write the final draft by looking at a section, see what you said, and say it better. Add, change, move, or delete sentences to improve the text. Ask others to read it and see if they understand what you mean. It may make sense to you, but you have to understand how others will see it.

You shouldn't be adding more ideas in the final draft. By having researched, outlined, and had the first draft reviewed by subject matter experts, you should have every idea in your first draft. If you find that you're adding new ideas to the final draft, you didn't do a complete job in your research, outlining, and first draft. Of course, you may add a few new items here and there.

This is the fun part of writing. Some people like to write on paper. Others like to type on screen. I've asked many writers and editors about this and opinions were roughly half for paper and half for digital. There's not a particular advantage to either one. It's up to you. I edit on paper. I print the chapters with 1.5 or double space and a wide right margin so there's room for notes. This means I can write anywhere, including on the sofa with the cat, on a long flight, in a hammock, and yes, in a café. When I'm done, I go to the computer and input the changes to the file.

When you finish, you send the final draft to the copyeditor, who edits for grammar, punctuation, and clarity. He doesn't review the content. He only fixes how you say it. You thought Miss Bluebird in high school was a hard teacher; she was nothing compared to how tough a good copyeditor can be.

The copyeditor sends his changes to you. Some copyeditors like to work with a pen on paper (they use red because they like it when your text bleeds); other copyeditors work on a digital version. Let them do it the way they like. They know grammar better than me, so I approve nearly all of their changes.

You don't need to have the complete final draft before you send it to the copyeditors. You can send chapters as they're ready. And they don't need to be in sequence. For some of my books, the copyeditors got the last chapters first, because those were the easy ones.

You need to find copyeditors. Don't hire someone who likes to read. I was lucky to know the people in the copyediting class at University of California at Berkeley, who did the copyediting on my book. You can find a list of those copyeditors at my book's webpage.

## Writing Styles and the Author's Voice

You can write in several styles: academic, business, or casual. Write in a style that's appropriate to your audience.

In the last few years, social media and blogging has affected business and professional writing. A casual sarcastic style is common. I've even heard *The New York Times* made a joke last year.

You have to be careful with jokes. A few jokes are fine, but it's hard to read a nonfiction book that's filled with jokes and sarcastic comments. Listen to your copyeditors. They'll let you know if a joke is okay, like my joke about the bear that... wait, the copyeditor deleted it. Okay, how about the jackrabbit in Texas..., no, that got deleted too.

You may wonder which writing techniques you can use to evoke emotions in your readers. No problem! Any author can easily get his readers bored or confused.

You can use the Flesch-Kincaid readability tool to measure the level complexity in your writing. Developed by the US Navy, it's included in Microsoft Word. To use this, do a spell check on your document. When it finishes, you can see your score. The higher the score, the better. Aim for 60-70 points. This book's score is 67.4. Learn more at Readability-Score.com.

How to Write a Book! by Andreas Ramos

The best rule is to keep it simple. If you avoid complex sentences, you won't confuse your readers or yourself.

Good writing is like a glass window. You see birds but not the glass.

## Content Freeze

After all of the changes have been made, you declare content freeze. That means no more changes. It's important that you stick to a content freeze. This lets people know when they must deliver. If you allow changes after the content freeze, writing turns into never-ending changes, rewrites, and edits.

## International English

Write in International English. This is the schoolbook English that's taught to kids in schools around the world. Write in short, declarative sentences. Use subject-verb-direct object sentence structure. Avoid too many clauses.

Don't use the active tense of a verb, such as, "I'm running to the store." Many readers in Germany or China don't really understand the difference between "I run to the store" and "I'm running to the store" because they don't have that verb form in their language.

Don't use Latin abbreviations, such as "e.g." and "i.e." or Roman numerals such as "XCIX." Many people (including many Americans) don't know what these mean.

If you write International English, it's easier to translate the text into another language.

## Should I Write in my Language or English?

People ask they should first write in their language and then translate to English. If you can write in English, do that because the market in English is worldwide. You won't have the additional work and expense of translation. Do your best in English. The copyeditors will clean up your grammar.

## What's the Hardest Part about Writing?

What's the hardest part of writing? Finishing! It's easy to start and it's easy to write a lot of pages. But it's very hard to edit, fix all of the last items, and getting the manuscript to production.

## I Want to Write, but I Don't Want to Read

You may notice by now that you'll read your manuscript many times. You write the notes. You read those and arrange them. You read the outline and drafts. You read the draft that you send to ten subject matter experts, who each send drafts to you so you read all ten. You send the final draft to your copyeditor, who makes changes, sends it back, and you read it again. After layout is done, you read it to check the layout. You also read it once last time before it goes to print. When you get the first printed book, you'll read it again.

I read my manuscripts perhaps thirty or forty times. After you've done this a few times, you'll have the entire book in your head; you'll know every sentence. When you get new ideas, you'll know exactly where to add them.

## The ARC: Advance Reading Copy

You can send an advance reading copy (ARC) to book reviewers at magazines and blogs. The ARC can be sent as a PDF. If you like, you can add a copyright message as a watermark to the ARC (a watermark is text that appears in pale grey behind the text).

## Editing the Final Draft

Your final draft should be as good as possible before you send it to your copyeditors. Here's my edit checklist (you can get a copy at the book's webpage):

- Make sure cell border lines in the tables are turned on
- Check heading text in all tables for consistent layout, font, and size
- Check cell text in all tables for consistent layout, font, and size
- Add space before and after every table
- Check the alignment of all tables
- Check the book title in the footer
- No bullet lists with only one single bullet
- Lists are alphabetized (if necessary)
- Steps in a process are numbered sequentially
- Check all web links to make sure they work
- Adjust the size and alignment of images
- Captions under the illustrations
- Use the word processor's spell check, but don't rely on it. It only shows the word is spelled correctly, but not if it's the wrong word. You'll have to read the text to make sure the words are correct.

## The Ideal Book Manuscript

Mukesh Jain, director of Jain Publishing, describes the ideal manuscript with the following characteristics:

- The text is well-written, clear, and concise. It communicates the idea to the reader.

- The material is well-organized: The front material, the body, and the back material is complete. The text is structured in logical segments.

- You did the research: You use citations in the proper format for your audience. Permissions for illustrations and included material are available.

- The text avoids gossipy remarks, arbitrary or personal judgments, unfounded speculation, or slander.

## The Copyeditor

When you have a clean text, you send it to the copyeditor. The copyeditor fixes punctuation, grammar, and sentence structure. The copyeditor also edits for clarity. She notes ambiguity or inconsistency. The copyeditor sends you author queries to ask you questions.

When you send drafts out for review, allow space on the page for comments, corrections, and additions by using a wide margins and double-space lines.

Decide on the level of editing. Do you want a light edit (fix only obvious errors), a medium edit (fix errors and occasional rewrite of sentences), or a heavy edit (rewrite the text)?

Good writers are comfortable with extensive changes to their text. I accept 98% of the copyeditor's changes. Don't refuse to delete sections or chapters if they say so. I've thrown out chapters because the copyeditor found these didn't support the main argument. It was great material, but not relevant. Listen to your copyeditor.

## What Happens If You Don't Work with Copyeditors?

If your text isn't reviewed by a copyeditor, it will be riddled with errors and that won't look good. If you ask friends to edit, they'll generally make a few minor changes. They don't know grammar and punctuation.

## How Do You Find Copyeditors?

If you self publish, you find your own developmental editor and copyeditor. If your book is produced by a publisher, the developmental editor, copyeditor, and others will be assigned to you.

Here are resources to find copyeditors:

- Bay Area Editors' Forum (BAEF) at EditorsForum.org

- Editcetera at Editcetera.com

- Editorial Freelancers Association (EFA) at The-EFA.org

You can also contact the copyeditors who worked on this book. They include: Gillian Bagwell (team leader) (GillianBagwell@hotmail.com), Isabelle Pouliot (Isabelle@desiu.ca), Jennifer Skancke (jen.skancke@gmail.com), Sean Morales (SeanFMorales@gmail.com), and Steven Nelson (SroyNelson@gmail.com).

## The Layout Draft

After you get the corrected final draft from the copyeditor, it goes to layout, which turns the manuscript into a document for printing. Layout includes the overall visual appearance of the book and the text, along with the white space on the page. Layout also makes sure there are no awkward line breaks at the top or bottom of a page. If necessary, text is added or deleted to improve the layout.

You should have a consistent layout and design for the entire book. This includes the cover, the text, and illustrations. Even better, the design should include the website, the newsletter, poster, and the ads.

The layout is the last step in production. Don't do layout before you've finished the final draft. Some people began to play with layout and they'll change it over and over as the text continues to change.

The layout depends on how the book will be read. Layout is different between printed books, PDFs, and ebooks.

- A printed book's page is smaller than a large tablet, so there's less text on the page. Footers and page numbers are necessary in printed books, but not digital books.

- PDFs are generally printed on A4 typewriter paper. This means you'll lay out the text as if it's for a printed book with a larger page size. Margins, headings, footer, and pagination should be adjusted. If the PDF will be printed in Europe, you must also adjust the layout for European paper sizes.

- Digital devices allow the reader to change fonts and adjust font size, which changes the layout. The layout person makes sure the book looks good after it has been resized on tablets and smart phones.

### *Layout for a Printed Book*

If you do the layout for a printed book or a PDF, here are some tips:

- You have control over the appearance of the page. This includes the font, size of font, margins, line breaks, and page breaks. This also includes spacing between letters, words, lines, and paragraphs. Fonts should be consistent in headings, paragraphs, and bullet points.

- Headings shouldn't start at the bottom of a page. Use a page break to move the heading to the next page.

- Paragraphs shouldn't end with a line with only one or two words. Adjust the text by adding or deleting text.

- Turn off hyphenation. Use ragged justification.

- A paragraph shouldn't have one or two lines on another page. Adjust the text as needed.

How to Write a Book! by Andreas Ramos

- Tables shouldn't break over two pages.

- Images should be at the top of a page and the caption should be under the image.

- Look for "rivers of white space." Rivers can be distracting. Adjust the text to break these up.

- Check the numbering in pagination, the table of content, chapter headings, numbered lists, and the index. Even if you used automated numbering, you have to manually check these because these tools can make mistakes.

The best way to do layout is to check each item one at a time. In the first pass, look at fonts. When you finish, go back, start again, and look at headings. Start again and look at paragraph endings. Go through the manuscript, over and over, and check each item on the list.

## Layout for an eBook

The layout for an ebook is different from print layout. First, your audience can read your ebook on many kinds of devices, including tablets such as Kindle, iPads, Nook, Kobo or smart phones such as iPhone, Samsung Galaxy, and so on. There are hundreds of mobile devices and more appear every day. Secondly, many devices allow your audience to change the font, type size, margins, line height, and even the font color.

So you don't have much control over layout. Think of your text as peanut butter and the ebook reader as a plastic tube. Your text flows into the tube. If you change the tube, you change the flow of the text.

There are only a few things for layout in ebooks:

- In general, keep the layout as simple as possible. Use chapter heading, section heading, body text, illustrations, and small simple table. The simpler, the better.

- You insert page breaks only at the start of a chapter. Don't adjust line breaks at the bottom of a page. The text flow will change when your reader adjusts his display settings.

- The table of contents is often placed at the end of the book (because most people ignore the table of content). You also shouldn't show page numbers (these don't matter in digital books). Amazon will make the table of contents clickable. When you set up the format for the table of contents, turn off page numbers, turn off "Right Align Page Numbers," and set the level to 2 (heading 2) or less. yyy

- The page numbers in the index can't be clicked. You can convert the index into a text file and add it to the book as a list of concepts. The page numbers in the index can't be clicked. You can convert the index into a text file and add it to the book as a list of concepts. You should also remove the indexing code. These are hidden tags such as { xe "Digital book" }. However, they're special code, so you have to use a special way to find them. Use Search/Replace and look for ^d xe ^? and replace them with a blank (no space).

- You should move the front matter to the back. This includes credits, acknowledgements, your author's biography, and so on. There's a reason for this. If Amazon sees someone gets your book via KDP or Amazon Unlimited and she reads more than 10% into the book, you get royalties. If she abandons your book before the 10% mark, you get nothing. So fill the first 10% with really good material to get her to read further. Upload your book to Amazon and look at the first 10% to make sure it's good material.

- If you have links in the text, Amazon will convert them into clickable links. However, your readers may click on links, go to another site, and forget your book.

- You don't need a footer (book title or page numbers).

- Tables often don't display properly. The easy solution is to show the information as a bullet list or make a screen shot of the table and insert it as an illustration.

When you upload your book to Amazon, you can use the previewer to look at the result. You can preview Kindle, Kindle Fire, iPad, and iPhone devices. Make any changes and upload a new file.

### Proofreading

Finally, the layout is sent to the proofreader. Most people think a proofreader checks for content or grammar. The copyeditor did that. The proofreader checks the changes by the developmental editor, the subject matter experts, and the copyeditors to make sure these are in the layout version.

### Summary of this Chapter

You rewrite the first draft to make a readable final draft. The final draft will be cleaned up by the copyeditors and made presentable by the layout person. The result is what your readers see.

# The Author Speaks: Mike Moran

Mike Moran co-authored a book with Bill Hunt (two editions) and one by himself. He and Bill are in the throes of the third edition and he's co-authoring another book with a different author. He writes about digital marketing, especially where technology and marketing come together. He focuses on issues that help marketers and technologists understand each other better, because companies won't make any money unless both groups work together to satisfy their customers. His books include *Search Engine Marketing, Inc.* (3rd ed., IBM Press, 2014) and *Do It Wrong Quickly: How the Web Changes the Old Marketing Rules* (IBM Press, 2007). Visit him at MikeMoran.com

### Why Do You Write?

I find that writing forces me to learn more about something that I start out thinking I'm an expert in. I teach for the same reason. I find the pressure of having to explain something in a simple way gets me reading and experimenting to be sure that I'm explaining it well.

### How Has Writing Affected Your Life and Career?

Writing a book can be excruciating because of the way it takes over my life. But writing has certainly been great for my career. It's helped me get speaking and consulting work, but it has also taught me a lot.

### Do You Prefer Self Publishing or Traditional?

Both of my books are published by Pearson, the world's largest publisher, so I haven't self published any of my own books yet. I did all the work to self publish my wife's book, so I know the drill, and in the right situation, self publishing might make sense.

### How Did You Find and Choose Your Publisher?

When Bill and I were thinking about our first book, I was working at IBM which has a deal with Pearson to publish employee books, so it wasn't a tough decision.

### What's Your Experience with Traditional Publishing?

The good is the publisher does all the work to produce and distribute the book, which is a lot of work. The bad is that it takes a few months to get that done and it's harder to keep the book up to date.

### Do You Have an Agent?

I don't have an agent. I once engaged a well-known agent to look over the contract that I negotiated and he said he couldn't do any better, so I couldn't come up with a reason to hire him.

### What's the Best Way to Promote Your Book?

I don't really think about it as ways to promote the book. To me, books, blogging, social media, speaking, consulting, and everything else just feeds each other. You never know how a new client will hear about you and it doesn't matter where they start.

### What Would You Have Done Differently?

I'd have written a book sooner. I had always wanted to do it but I kept letting other things get in the way.

# 6. Working with a Copyeditor

This chapter is by Lisa Carlson, who teaches copyediting at UC Berkeley Extension. Lisa arranged the copyediting of this book. Hilary Powers also assisted in developing this chapter.

## Why You Need a Copyeditor

No matter how great a writer you may be, you need a copyeditor. As stated earlier, a copyeditor corrects basic errors of punctuation, grammar, spelling, logic, and style, queries the author, and prepares a style sheet, among other things. Together, you and your copyeditor decide if your book needs a light, medium, or heavy copyedit.

## Finding a Copyeditor

Meet your copyeditor. Find out about their work background, how long they've been copyediting, and what kinds of projects they've worked on. Discuss your budget and the copyeditor's rates. Many factors can affect your cost for copyediting, such as:

- Do you need this in a few days or a couple of months?

- A heavy copyedit will cost more than a light edit.

- Your level of involvement: Will you want the copyeditor to meet often with you or can they work on their own?

- The level of complexity: Is the text complex or specialized? Are there a lot of figures, graphs, or illustrations?

- Location: Expect to pay more in Silicon Valley or New York than in the Midwest.

Show the copyeditor your manuscript. Get their feedback on your writing style. Tell them about your hopes for the book. Discuss the intended audience. Talk about how you prefer to work: do you want edits on paper or electronically? Is your computer software compatible with your copyeditor's? Do you want to share files in the Cloud? Using Google Docs? Is there a style sheet for the book, or do you want your copyeditor to create one? Should they base their work on the *Chicago Manual of Style*, the *AP Stylebook*, or another well-known style guide, such as *AMA Manual of Style* for medical books?

Working style and subject matter knowledge will also enter the picture. If your book is about the future of technology but the copyeditor has only edited books on spirituality, that can be a problem. So, try to match the kind of book you've written with the copyeditor's background and experience.

## *Working through the Manuscript*

Decide on a timeline. Will the copyeditor send you their work when the entire book has been edited or by chapter? Are you open to receiving author queries early in the game? This can help the copyeditor immensely, as, with several key questions addressed early on and already answered, the copyeditor can concentrate on doing the actual editing with the new information included.

How many drafts do you want from the copyeditor? Two drafts are standard, but you may need more passes, depending on the quality of your writing. Will the copyeditor also be expected to proof the final draft, or will you hire a proofreader?

The first draft from the copyeditor will have queries, comments, and suggestions for deletions or requests for additional content to clarify, in addition to correction of all grammar, spelling, punctuation, usage, and style errors. A good copyeditor will strive to maintain your voice as author, but may also improve it. If the tone is casual, the editor shouldn't change that, but should improve the quality of the language. Expect the author to flag or correct any inconsistencies in your manuscript. In a light copyedit you usually won't see any sentences recast, but in a medium copyedit, there will be some rephrasing of sentences, perhaps to simplify them, or to avoid use of passive voice. In a heavy copyedit, expect a rigorous scrub of your work, and that may also mean reorganization of paragraphs for improved flow and logic, with line edits to improve the writing overall.

And now, for the hard part: It's up to you to respond to all queries as quickly as possible. As mentioned above, sometimes this can be done while the copyeditor is working on the first draft, but you'll usually address queries after receiving the first draft. If the manuscript has been marked up on paper, you'll clearly see all the copyeditor's decisions on the page, and you can approve them or disagree with them. If the copyeditor has edited electronically using the Track Changes feature, you can read the manuscript in Final view, which shows you the clean copy after editing, and you can also change the setting to view each edit. The queries may appear within the text or as separate, numbered comments along the side of the electronic manuscript or as a numbered list underneath the text, depending on how you apply your software settings. Additionally, your copyeditor will provide a cover letter listing all the work they've done and general tips on how to improve your writing.

Expect all copyeditors to flag redundancy (you said it twice or more, for no apparent reason), verbosity (you used too many words to say something simple), use of trite phrases, hackneyed expressions, and clichés. Using a style sheet, the copyeditor will expect precision regarding dates, unusual name spellings, geographical locations, foreign words, and graphs, charts, and figures. The copyeditor should do research, but they'll also either mark up the content, or ask you to verify information, or ask you to do further fact checking. For a complex project, consider hiring a fact checker.

Once you review and return the copyedited manuscript, the editor will make all edit entries and finalize the text, making it look as professional and clean on the page as possible. At this point the copyeditor will also finalize the glossary and index. If your book has a complex index, you can also hire an indexer.

Following the layout of the entire book and prior to printing, a proofreader will compare the corrected final layout to page proofs. You may want to hire someone who was not the copyeditor to do this. Always give this person the style sheet and any additional background information that can help them.

## What You Give to the Copyeditor

Give the copyeditor as much background information about the writing project as you can, in addition to your manuscript draft. Is this a family history based on your research with a genealogist and interviews with your aunt Selma? Did your travels across the American landscape to unearth your ancestral roots inform the book? Do you think your copyeditor could benefit from knowing some of the back story to your writing? Of course it would be helpful to the copyeditor! Unless you plan to spend a lot of time discussing your writing over coffee and lunch with your copyeditor, supplying them with supporting materials and notes can ease and inform the editing process for them. This includes:

- A complete manuscript, double-spaced, in an easy-to-read 12-point font and page numbering.

- Supporting materials for your project, such as a style sheet, interviews, images, websites, or background notes.

- A nondisclosure agreement to be signed by you and the copyeditor, ensuring the contents remain confidential prior to your book's publication.

## How Long Should Copyediting Take?

It can take a few weeks or several years, depending on the manuscript. The ideal is somewhere in between, even in this world of constantly accelerating change and instant everything. For example, *I Hotel*, by Karen Tei Yamashita, was published in 2010 by Coffee House Press, a small Minneapolis publisher. The 600-page novel had an inordinate number of layout issues, based on special graphics and illustrations. It took nearly three years from delivery to publication.

As an independent copyeditor working with a new author, I once spent nearly a year copyediting a novel. The dyslexic author was not good at spelling, and there was a lot of cutting to be done to bring the novel down to average book length. An exciting thriller emerged at the end, but our work really did require a lot of handholding, many meetings, and three editing passes before I turned over the final copyedited manuscript.

Ideally, if the book isn't too long and a medium edit is required, without a lot of complex illustrations, photos, or charts and figures, three to four weeks of copyediting for two passes should suffice.

Most seasoned copyeditors can copyedit about four pages an hour at a medium level of editing. It's less time-consuming to do a light edit, and a heavy edit may require more time (maybe a page or two per hour). If there are figures, it takes at least a separate two passes for the editor to review those. Graphics and photography add yet another level of complexity.

## The Copyeditor Gives You...

The first items to expect from your chosen copyeditor are:

- A proposal: The copyeditor should send a proposal or work plan. This should tell you how the copyeditor plans to approach editing your manuscript. They'll usually write this up after asking you questions about the project and your expectations about the outcome.

- A budget: How much will the copyeditor charge you? This can be a flat fee, an hourly rate, or an amount per page.

## You Give the Copyeditor

You should also give a few things to your copyeditor:

- Glossary of terms and acronyms: This is a list of words or business jargon and definitions, usually only required for technical books or insider books.

- The style sheet: Manuscripts longer than a few pages usually require a style sheet. This gives everyone in the book project the agreed-upon and correct spellings for names and places, decisions on usage (will numbers be spelled out or will they appear in Arabic? Should measurements use the metric system? Will certain spellings be in British style vs. U.S. style?) and other style choices, such as use of hyphenation, treatment of bulleted lists, capitalization rules for headers, and other editorial decisions.

- Description of the audience: Is the book intended for academics, sales people, engineers, or students?

- Purpose of the book: Is your intention to counsel, instruct, inform, inspire, entertain, or all of the above?

- Description of the book: Will it be scientific or academic, a textbook, or a how-to guide?

## What the Copyeditor Delivers

Your copyeditor will deliver a cover letter addressing any additional issues or concerns they have about the book and publication. This will accompany a readable, typo-free, grammatically correct, copyedited book. The layout should be clean, the pages numbered, the figures correct, the graphic elements clean, and all points of style and queries will have been addressed. There should be a table of contents, and if needed, an index. Front matter , such as title page, copyright page, forward, and table of contents; and back matter, such as the bibliography, references, a glossary, and an index will be included.

## A Contract for Your Copyeditor

You'll also need a contract or letter of agreement with your copyeditor. This spells out the deliverables, scope of work, timeline, and the fee. Here's an example (a copy is at this book's webpage):

This is an agreement between _____ ("The Client") located at _____ (address), and _____ ("The Copyeditor") located at _____ (address), for copyediting the book, _____ (Working Title).

The client has hired the editor to revise the current book for a fee of $_____. The fee will be paid 50% on start and 50% on delivery. The project starts on _____ (date). Final delivery will be on _____ (date).

Should additional copyediting be necessary for the scope of work changes during the course of this assignment, the above terms will be renegotiated by the two parties and a new written agreement will be signed.

The Copyeditor acknowledges and agrees that all material submitted by the Client is and will remain the property of the Client. Further, the Copyeditor will not give or in any way transfer the material to a third party without written permission of the Client.

The Copyeditor also acknowledges and agrees that this editing work is paid for on a fee for services basis, and the Copyeditor will have no claim of any sort on edited material, subsequent manuscript and/or book or part thereof, including but not limited to proceeds from its sale.

Agreed and accepted:

Client: _____ Date: _____
Copyeditor: _____ Date: _____

## Arguing with Your Copyeditor

The copyeditor may not always be right, but, if the person is professional, they know the rules. If you come across an editorial mark on your manuscript that you disagree with, feel free to ask the copyeditor why it's there. The editor should be able to cite a rule, such as Chicago 6.18 (which refers to a paragraph in the Chicago Manual of Style) or provide a reason for the decision.

Well-known authors frequently argued with their editors. Sometimes it was about voice or character, style, or concision and length. F. Scott Fitzgerald, Ernest Hemingway, and Thomas Wolfe worked with famed editor Maxwell Perkins, who had to deal with their eccentricities and personalities. His skill that helped make them into the writers we know today. Raymond Carver worked with copyeditor Gordon Lish at Esquire Magazine who deleted enormous amounts of text to bring out the essence of Carver's stories. A New Yorker article shows before-and-after changes (see http://goo.gl/wbs7Cu).

## An Example of a Copyediting Project

A client once came to me with a proposal for a book about interior decorating using African influences. The proposal needed editing, so I spent about a month on the project, which included counseling my client about writing, sharpening two sample chapters, and developing the book proposal. I accompanied her to a meeting with her agent. It quickly became clear the format was not correct and the agent felt, after considering her list of likely publishers, that she'd have a hard time selling this book. My client and I took notes and we went back to the drawing board. I became a collaborator as well as a copyeditor. It took another month, and we emerged with a more focused proposal and tightly copyedited text. We were so thrilled and excited at the prospect of seeing this book come alive! Too bad, because the proposal was rejected again. The agent felt the market for the book was not there.

So, on we marched to another agent, with the same proposal, and this new agent loved it. Within a few weeks, a publisher expressed interest in the manuscript. But the publisher wanted the book to be refocused: instead of interior decorating, they saw a broader market for a book

How to Write a Book! by Andreas Ramos

about how to entertain, African-American style with décor, style, recipes, interviews, and more. My client went back to work, doing additional research, and revising the proposal, which I copyedited. The book was sold, my client wrote it over a six-month period, and, based on providing her with two edited drafts, I had guaranteed employment from this project alone, for nearly a year!

Now, as an author, you may be wondering, do I have the stamina to go through all these phases of preliminary work before getting my book accepted by a publisher? Could I cover my copyeditor's fees for that amount of time? Well, that's one reason there's now such a huge self-publishing business out there – because most new authors don't want to go through these iterations at the whim of a potential publisher. But, that aside, one of the things my client learned during this sequence of events, was how valuable it could be for her to have a collaborative copyeditor who responded to her book project vision, and who stayed with her throughout the rigorous process, all the way to final edited draft and publication.

The book was published and released in time for Thanksgiving. It sold well and was re-issued in paperback about a year later, then again the following year. This time the publisher was right: by broadening the target audience the book became timeless, in a sense – it could be reissued year after year for the holidays and still attract new readers and bring in profits. My client has been forever grateful to me for my copyediting, and over a decade later, we're embarking on a new project together.

## Conclusion

Now you know what a copyeditor does, how to find one, work with one, and bring your final manuscript to the world, whether you work with a publisher or take on self publishing. If you still have questions about the process of editing, I recommend that you read *The Copyeditor's Handbook* by Amy Einsohn. Written to instruct and train copyeditors, it's also a wonderful guide about the editorial process for the new author. Reading this book will help you work with a copyeditor, gain insight into how editors think, and bring you additional appreciation for the field of editing.

## *Top Rules from the Chicago Manual of Style*

- Put punctuation (periods, commas, and so on) inside quotation marks. She said, "I want ice cream."

- If a question is within quotation marks, the question mark goes inside the quotation marks. She asked, "Will you call?"

- Start quotation marks with commas. She said, "Let's go!"

- If the sentence stands alone, put punctuation inside the parentheses. (We have a cat.) If the sentence is part of the main sentence, put the period outside the parenthesis. We have two pets (I forgot about our bird).

- Spell out large numbers, such as one hundred thousand. Be consistent in how you show numbers.

- Don't start sentences with a numeral. Spell it out.

- Spell out "%" as "percent." Use the "%"in graphs and charts.

- Spell out Fahrenheit or Celsius for temperatures.

- After a colon: lowercase the first word. However, if there are more sentences, use a capital letter, as in: Use a capital letter. There are more sentences to follow.

- If you use a foreign word, put it in italics.

- Don't use scare quotes. If the writing is good, the emphasis will be understood. Otherwise, use italics to emphasize.

- Don't underline.

- Don't use periods in headings or subheadings.

- Italicize book titles (but not if it's a book series). Use quotation marks for the title of an article.

- Self-publish has a hyphen when it modifies a noun. "Self-published books are big." Don't hyphenate if it stands alone, for example, "He will self publish."

- Use serial commas. "I have a cat, a dog, and a bird."

How to Write a Book! by Andreas Ramos

## *A Few More Good Rules*

- Use a consistent writing style.

- Don't use jargon, clichés, and tired phrases.

- Write in active voice. Don't write, "the mouse was chased by the cat." Write, "the cat chased the mouse."

- Don't repeat "the" in a list. For example, "they brought the iPad, the iPhone, and the toaster…" should be, "They brought the iPad, iPhone, and toaster."

- Spell out acronyms in parentheses upon first use. "I sent an ARC (advance reading copy)."

- Avoid metadiscourse. Don't refer to the text ("I will explain, show, suggest, summarize…"), the writer's attitude ("it seems, perhaps"), the reader's action ("as you might recall, consider now"), or the writing itself ("finally, however"). By avoiding metadiscourse, your writing becomes direct.

- Don't use a question mark if you're making a statement about a question.

- If a bulleted list has a sentence, use a period at the end of every line for consistency.

- Be concise.

- Read your text aloud. Listen for anything that may sound off or could be misunderstood by a casual reader.

These are rules for American English. There are differences for UK English and other languages.

# 7. The Parts of Your Book

What makes up a book? Here is a quick chapter on the parts of a book. Let's start at the front of a nonfiction book and go through it:

- **Front Cover**: The front cover has the book's title, your name, the publisher's logo, and an illustration. Technical books may have a few bullet points to describe the book. If the book has won awards, these may appear on the cover. The cover's design is important because it attracts potential readers to pick up the book. I recommend a trained graphics designer should make your cover.

- **Spine**: The spine is the side of the book that connects the front and back cover. It should also match the cover design.

- **The Front Matter**: The front matter (FM) is the first few pages of information about the book, such as the title page, copyright notice, foreword, preface, and the dedication page.

- **Title Page**: The title page states the title, subtitle, and the author's name.

- **Copyright Notice**: The copyright notice declares the legal owner of the book.

- **Foreword**: The foreword is a one-page introduction to the book, often by a leading person in your field. Ask someone at the beginning of your project to write the introduction and give them a firm deadline; they're busy and it can take eight weeks to write one page.

- **Preface**: The preface may be one or two pages where you explain why you wrote the book. You can also add acknowledgements to thank the people who helped you with the book.

How to Write a Book! by Andreas Ramos

- **Dedication**: There may also be a single page with a dedication, such as, "For Lao Por & Xiao Mao." You can dedicate your book to your partner, your friends, or your cat. Don't skip this. It means a lot to them. Okay, your cat won't care. My wife Helen is flattered but I still have to clean the garage.

- **One-page Summary**: This is a one-page summary of each chapter of the book on a single page. It helps your reader choose what to read (or ignore).

- **Table of Contents (TOC)**: The table of contents is a list of the chapters and sections in the book. It may include chapter headings, section headings, and sub-headings. This should be two or three pages. The table of contents isn't just a list. Your reader should be able to read the table of contents.

- **Chapters**: A book is made up of chapters. The chapters should develop the idea of the book.

- **Opening Summary for each Chapter**: Each chapter should start with a short one-paragraph summary of what the chapter will cover. You could also use bullet points. The summary allows people to see if they want to read the chapter.

- **Conclusion for each Chapter:** Just like the opening summary, the chapter should also end with a summary. This helps people understand what they just read.

- **Headings and Sub-headings**: Within the chapter, use headings and sub-headings. Headings serve to organize and announce the content. Don't use more than two levels. People may lose track of the main idea.

- **Body Text**: Remember those long hours in high school on how to write? A paragraph isn't just a bunch of words. A paragraph starts with a statement, adds several sentences to explain or expand the statement, and ends with a conclusion. A sentence makes sense on its own. A paragraph also makes sense as a whole.

- **Illustrations:** There are several purposes for illustrations. A drawing can often explain an idea better than text, especially if you're describing spatial or sequential ideas. Illustrations also break up the text so your readers don't get bored. Try to put an illustration every four pages. You should also add captions under the illustrations. People read the captions before they read the body text.

- **Conclusion for the Book**: The conclusion is your short one- or two-page summary of the book. Restate the main argument of the book, explain why it matters, and offer what you think may come next.

- **The Back Matter**: Just as the front matter has information about the book, the back matter (BM) also contains additional information, including references, bibliography, contact information, index, and a glossary.

- **References**: The references page has additional useful information, such as a list of resources, other books, conferences, blogs, and websites. Don't just give a list: add your comments on why it's important or useful.

- **Contact**: You can also include a contact section with your email address, website address, and newsletter subscription information.

- **Index**: The index is a list of key terms in the book, along with the page numbers where the terms can be found.

- **Additional Pages**: You can also add additional pages, such as notices for other books by you.

- **Back Cover**: The back cover often has your photo and a short description about you. It may also have bullet points that tell the reader what they'll get out of the book. The design of the back cover should match the front cover. The back cover may also have an ISBN number and bar code.

Let's look at some of these in more detail.

## The Working Title and the Book's Title

While you're writing the book, you have a working title, which is what you really think the book is about.

When you publish the book, it gets a new title. This is the title for the public. It has to say what the book is about but it also has to give the reader a reason to pick up the book. It should appeal to your reader and make them curious about what's inside.

If you work with a publisher, they decide the title. You may suggest a title, but they decide. It can be amusing to compare authors' working titles and the published title. Harper Lee's *To Kill a Mockingbird* was originally titled *Atticus.* George Orwell's *Nineteen Eighty-Four* started as *The Last Man in Europe.* John Steinbeck's *Of Mice and Men* was *Something That Happened.*

For this book, my working title was *Write a Book.*

By the way, there is no copyright on titles. You can name your book whatever you want. Yes, you can use *Gone with the Wind*, but that may create confusion, so it's better to give your book a unique title.

## Use Google Keyword Planner for Your Book Title

You can research keywords with Google Adwords' Keyword Planner. This is free at Google. Along with ideas for keywords, it also includes the number of monthly searches for the keyword. Many people may have their ideal keyword, but if nobody searches for it, it's a useless keyword. Look for keywords with substantial searches (10,000 or more). To use this:

- Go to Google Adwords | Tools | Keyword Planner | Search for New Keyword and Ad Group Ideas. (To use this, you must have an Adwords account. But you don't need to pay for it. Set up the account but don't add a credit card. To learn how to set up and manage Google Adwords, see the chapter on Google Adwords in my book *Search Engine Marketing*).

- Add a list of keywords, one per line

- Select the country

- Click the Keywords Ideas tab
- Sort the table by Avg. Monthly Searches to see the number of monthly searches, averaged over the last twelve months

Here are results for my keyword research at Google Adwords. After each keyword phrase (in italics), I included the number of monthly searches for that phrase, averaged over a year: *write your book* (has zero searches), *write my book* (zero), *write books* (110), *write a book* (3,600), *writing a book* (12,600), *how to write a book* (49,500), *how to publish a book* (18,000), *how to get published* (2,400), *how to write books* (260).

You can see the most obvious keywords aren't the ones with the best traffic. Nobody searches for *Write Your Book* in the Google search engine, but *how to write a book* has 49,500 searches. Which one should be the title?

You can also see it's not obvious without checking Google. *How to write a book* (49,500 monthly searches) and *how to write books* (260 monthly searches) are nearly the same, yet the first has 49,500 monthly searches and the second has 260 monthly searches.

You can do the same for the subtitle. Check to see which keywords resonate best with your audience. A long sub-title lets you explain your book's key idea and you can add more keywords to the title.

Here are examples of keywords for a subtitle: *career* (200,000), *job* (550,000), *professional* (200,000), *profession* (135,000), *work* (247,000).

For more ideas for book titles, look in Amazon. Search for your topic and then sort the books by Avg. Customer Review and Most Reviews. You'll see which titles get the most attention.

As I was writing *The Big Book of Content Marketing*, the working title was *Content Marketing*. I asked the team for suggestions and they came up with 25 titles. I created a Google Adwords campaign with 25 banner ads, one for each title, and tried all of them to see which one got the most clicks. The winner was *The Big Book of Content Marketing*.

Figure 4: The title for *The Big Book of Content Marketing* was selected by testing the number of clicks on banner ads for 25 titles.

## Designing the Book Cover

People say you shouldn't judge a book by its cover, but that's what people do. Your cover plays a great part in the success or failure of your book. The purpose of the cover is to get someone to notice your book.

The cover should match the theme of the book. The cover should also look professional. Mark Coker of Smashwords says, "The cover should deliver on the emotional promise of the book."

Along with an image, the cover should have the book's title, the author's name, the publisher's logo, and any awards or blurbs.

You can either buy a cover or you can have someone make it for you. There are plenty of websites that sell book covers. To find those, search for something like "get a cover for my book." You can also find cover designers at eLance.com, Freelancer.com, or ODesk.com. It's $25 to $500 for a cover.

If you didn't go to art school, I strongly suggest you don't do this yourself. It'll look amateurish and your sales will suffer.

Make sure that your designer has experience with book covers. The cover has to look good in various sizes: postage stamp, a book cover, and a poster (3 feet or 1 meter tall). If you publish at Amazon, it must meet specific horizontal and vertical sizes (Amazon will reject a cover that's a single pixel wrong). Ask to see covers the designer has done for other authors.

Designers often don't want you to give them covers from other books. It may influence their design and you'll end up with a cover that looks like your competitor's book. In the few cases when I made suggestions, the designer ignored me and the results were better. Generally, I ask the designer to come up with three or four sketch ideas. We pick one and go with that. The design can be pretty challenging. For the content marketing book, the designer made more than 25 covers.

If you work with a publisher, you may suggest, but they decide.

## The Index

The index helps your reader to find information in your book. You should anticipate the terms your reader will want to find. For example, look for *Facebook* in the index and see it's discussed on page 34 and 42.

An index is more than a list of the words in the book. It also includes ideas and concepts. The index may tell you the concept of social media is covered with mentions of Facebook, LinkedIn, and Twitter.

Some people argue you don't need an index on digital devices because you can use the search function to find any word. Yes, that's true if the word appears in the text. But this won't find concepts. People will use the index months later to find something they read about, but can't remember the exact words.

The index should also include names of key people in your field because they'll often look up themselves.

Here's how to make an index. Print the final manuscript. Use a highlighter pen and go through the manuscript several times. In the first pass, you look for names of people and companies. In the second pass, you look for general concepts. In the third pass, you look at illustrations. And so on.

How to Write a Book! by Andreas Ramos

Here are the things to put in an index:

- Names of people and companies

- Titles of software and books

- Chapter headings and major sections

- Paragraph topics

- Important concepts

- Examples

- How to perform a task

- Features and benefits of products or services

- Acronyms and abbreviations

- Tables

- Illustrations

In general, an index should about 5% of the book. If the book has 100 pages, the index should be an additional five pages.

You need to edit the index. Review every entry carefully. Make sure sub-topics are placed under their general heading. Before you publish, refresh the index to update entries and page numbers. With Microsoft Word, place the cursor in the index and press F9 to refresh the index.

An index shows professional attention. Books without indexes or a single-page index are generally rush jobs by non-professionals. Some publishers cut costs by omitting the index. If you work with a good publisher, they'll make an index. If you self publish, you make the index. You can index a book in an afternoon.

## *What about Footnotes?*

You can also include footnotes (at the bottom of a page) or endnotes (at the end of a chapter). You should use these if your book is for academic or scholarly publication. However, most business books don't use footnotes or endnotes. Look at books by major publishers in your field to see the standard.

## The Numbers: ISBN, ASIN, BISAC, and Bar Codes

The International Standard Book Number (ISBN) is an inventory number that allows publishers, book distributors, and book stores to keep track of books. The ISBN number for my book by McGraw-Hill is ISBN 978-0071597333.

Carla King points out you should buy and register your own ISBN. If you allow publishers to assign the ISBN, they control your book's distribution. Read her book *Self-Publishing Boot Camp* for more on this.

If you buy an ISBN, then buy ten for $250; it's cheaper and easier. You need an ISBN for each version of your book: print, Kindle, Nook, PDF.

If you publish your book with Smashwords, they'll assign a free ISBN.

Amazon will assign a free Amazon Standard Inventory Number (ASIN). The ASIN for my content marketing book is B00D1C3KJC..

The Book Industry Study Group uses BISAC codes to book categories. This book is in Business & Economics; Business Writing with BISAC BUS011000. At Amazon, you can assign a BISAC code. See BISG.org.

If you're going to sell in a bookstore, you'll need a bar code. This is the ISBN number encoded as bars to allow scanners to read the ISBN. Services on the web will convert your ISBN into a bar code.

If you don't expect to sell your book in bookstores, you don't need an ISBN or bar code for your book.

An ISBN, ASIN, or BISAC isn't the same as a copyright. These are just inventory tracking numbers. You register a copyright with the US government (more on this in the chapter on legal issues).

## Summary of this Chapter

I listed the parts of a book, but this doesn't mean you must use every one. It depends on your topic and audience. Look at leading books in your field, especially by major publishers, to see what they did.

# 8. Tools for Writing

## Introduction

This chapter covers the things I find useful for writing. These include the computer, monitor, keyboard, and software.

## Write with a Pen or on a Keyboard?

Let's start with the pen. I know writers who write with a pen. It works. But I find it's easier to write on a computer. The computer lets you move paragraphs and sentences. Your text software also has features that pen and paper can't match, such as outline view, dynamic table of content, and dynamic indexing. Nevertheless, if you want to write with a pen, that's fine. Use whatever works for you.

Does anyone really still write by hand? Joyce Carol Oates, Neil Gaiman, Amy Tan, and Jhumpa Lahiri write their books by hand.

Many writer also write on typewriters, including Cormac McCarthy, Danielle Steel, P.J. O'Rourke, Tom Wolfe, Will Self, Don DeLillo, and Frederick Forsyth.

## Which Computer?

It doesn't really matter if you use Windows or Apple. Either is fine. If you control the entire process from writing to layout, you can use whatever you like.

In my experience, you should use one or the other. If some people in your team use Windows and others use Mac, problems may arise as you transfer files back and forth.

## The Keyboard

Figure 5: A standard keyboard layout. Image by Peter Schlömer.

Most computer keyboards are made for casual typing of emails or short documents. Nearly all desktop keyboards are too light. Those keyboards only cost $10, which means these are junk keyboards. Laptop keyboards are narrow, which forces your wrists together. This position puts strain on your arms and wrists, which may result in repetitive stress injury (RSI).

I suggest you get a professional keyboard. The mechanics of the keys and their placement allows you to type easier and faster. I use the Model S Professional keyboards from DasKeyboard.com (about $100 for a keyboard).

A keyboard tray goes under your desk and holds the keyboard. You can adjust to the height and angle for your hands. Search for ergonomic keyboard tray.

An alternative to typing is dictation to a tape recorder or digital recorder. Several services will transcribe your recording to text. You can also use Dragon voice recognition (by Nuance.com). Several friends use this and they like it,

## Use a Big Screen

Use a large screen or two side-by-side monitors. This lets you open three or four documents so you can copy and paste from one to another. It's very hard to do this on a laptop. You can't do this on a tablet. Get the largest screen you can afford.

How to Write a Book! by Andreas Ramos

To use two screens with a desktop computer, you need a graphics card that has two monitor ports for screens. These graphic cards are fairly inexpensive (under $40) and any computer repair shop or your neighbor's 14-year old can do this for you. (Really, you can do this yourself. See the connection at the back of your computer where your monitor is connected? That's the graphics card. Unplug the power cords. Open the computer. Undo a few screws. Jiggle the graphics card until it comes out. Put the new card in the same place. Replace the screws and connect the monitors).

## *Software for Writing*

I prefer Word, but it's not the only software. You can write in Adobe Framemaker, Scrivener, Apache OpenOffice, NeoOffice, or other tools. In the following, I'll talk about Word, but much of this also applies to the other programs.

Microsoft Word has many useful tools for writing. For example, it can insert a table of contents. If you use formatting styles, which means you assign a format style to headings, then you can place the cursor to insert a table of content for the entire book. It's easy to update when you make changes. I was visiting a friend at Stanford who was working on her 250-page doctoral thesis. She was busy writing a new table of contents because the manuscript had gone through committee review and many sections were moved or deleted so the page numbering changed. It would take her several days to do this by hand. I said, "Hey, move over. Let me try something." I made a copy of the document and deleted the hand-edited table of contents. She yelled, "OMG! You deleted it!" I instantly generated a new, up-to-date table of contents. She was shocked to realize how much time she had lost.

Be sure to use Word's AutoCorrect feature. It automatically corrects misspelled words as you type. If it doesn't know your misspelling, the word is underlined in red. You click and it suggests possible spellings. You select the correct spelling and it will fix that mistake in the future. People tend to repeat the same spelling mistakes, so after a while, it will learn most of your mistakes. This saves a great deal of time. You can just type and not worry about spelling.

If you switch to a new computer, or you write on several computers, you can combine your spelling dictionaries. If you go through the trouble of finding and fixing spelling mistakes, you should be able to carry that work to your new computer or another computer.

To do this, open your spelling dictionary, copy it, save it as a text file, and paste it into the other computer. The dictionary is an ordinary text file. You can open your spelling dictionary by opening a file browser and pasting the following path: C:\Users\(your name)\AppData\Roaming\Microsoft\Proof\CUSTOM.DIC in the path line, where (your name) is whatever you use for your name on your computer. For example, the path on my computer is C:\Users\Andreas\AppData\Roaming\Microsoft\Proof\CUSTOM.DIC. Open the dictionary file, copy it, and save it as a text file. You may want to review it and make any changes. In the other computer, open the dictionary file and paste the text file.

Be careful with the word processor's grammar tool. It fixes obvious mistakes, but no software will fix unclear thinking. Be sure to work with copyeditors and subject matter experts.

You can also set Word to make automatic backups. I set mine to sixty seconds.

Most people use only a small part of Word. It has style editor, macros, and many other capabilities. Get a book on Word and learn how to use it. There are many books on Word but it's difficult to make a recommendation, since it depends on your level of computer expertise. In general, *Visual QuickStart* books by Peachpit Press are very good.

What about other writing tools? Framemaker is popular with technical writers. For years, there was a running debate among tech writers over which was better for professional writing. I was the tech pubs manager at a large database company, so I decided to settle the issue. I had to produce computer manuals for servers in Windows and UNIX, so I assigned the project to two writers where one used Word and the other used Framemaker. We then published the manuals. I showed both manuals to tech writers and asked which was made with which? They couldn't tell. Word, when used properly, can produce excellent professional results.

There are also collaboration tools that allow a group of people to work on a document together. Kintone, the top collaboration tool from Japan, lets you share files, post group messages, work flow management, and more. More at Kintone.com.

## Use Styles and Hot Keys

This book uses format styles for chapter headings, section headings, body text, and bullet points. Each one is defined by a format style. For example, the style setting for section headings is Trebuchet font in 12 points, with 5 points leading and 3 points following.

You define the settings for the style. You should also turn the auto-update feature, so if you make a change to the style, it's automatically updated throughout the manuscript. Finally, you assign the style to a combination of keys. This lets you write a line and then press Control and a function key to turn it into a chapter heading, section heading, body text, or a bullet list.

Hot keys, also called accelerator keys, let you make format changes. You can change the layout of hundreds of pages with a key press.

The importance of format styles can't be overstated. If you don't use styles, you'll waste a time in preparing the text for layout. You can't create dynamically-generated table of contents or indexes. Finally, if you upload your file without styles to Smashwords or Amazon, the text will be rejected. Go ahead and learn how to use and modify styles.

## Adobe InDesign for Layout

Adobe InDesign, as the name implies, is a layout tool. You copy text into it and use it to do the layout. It's widely used by publishers for book layout.

If you work with a publisher, they'll likely convert your Word file into an InDesign file. Once this happens, you can't make updates to the Word file. The book is out of your hands. If you self publish, you can use Word or Framemaker to write and lay out the book. You don't need InDesign.

I wrote the content marketing book in Word on a PC and the layout was done with InDesign on Apple Macintosh. However, when we moved the file from Windows Word to Mac InDesign, hundreds of errors happened in hyphenation and line breaks. This took days to fix.

## Illustrations for Your Book

You should use illustrations in your book. This can be drawings, charts, diagrams, or photographs.

There are plenty of sites where you can get images for your book. Wikimedia has many copyright-free images which can be used by anyone for anything. Go to commons.wikimedia.org.

You can also hire illustrators for cover design or illustrations. If you get someone to do graphics work for you, use a work-for-hire contract that gives you the ownership of the work so you can use it for posters, flyers, etc. You can get a copy of a contract at Andreas.com. To find illustrators, go to eLance.com, ODesk.com, or Freelancer.com.

Be sure to check the image's copyright status to make sure you have permission to use the image. It's common for people to take images from the web to use in their slide presentations, but you can't do this for books for publication, since it's considered commercial use. You should comply with the image's legal ownership. Otherwise, you may be liable for copyright infringement. You should keep these signed documents in your archives.

If you're working with a publisher, your publisher will ask you to provide copies of signed permission for each illustration. If a publisher prints your book, he'll ask for indemnification in the contract, which means if you steal illustrations and someone sues, the publisher will point the lawyer to you.

Here are several things to consider when working with illustrations:

- If you use photos of people, you need for them to sign a *Model Release Form*. This gives you permission to use their image. If you use photos of children, the child's parent or guardian should sign the Model Release Form. If you take a photo of a group of people, you need signed permission from each person. You can get a copy of the model release form at the webpage for this book.

- If you misuse copyrighted illustrations, drawings, or photographs, the holder of the rights can bring legal action against you. Some photographers have gotten millions of dollars from companies which used their work without permission.

- It can be complicated if you use photos of actors, politicians, or business people. In some cases, they're public figures and they can expect their image will be used. But you can't use their photo to promote your products. Discuss this with people who have experience with this.

- If you use your own images and you want to make sure others aren't using them, use TinEye.com to search for copies of your images.

Every illustration, screenshot, drawing, or photograph should have a caption. People read the captions before they read the text. If it's interesting, they'll read the rest of the page. So write good captions. You should also make it obvious that it's a caption. For example, I add "Figure 22" to the caption. The number is automated in my template, so when you add new illustrations, the numbers are updated.

Many authors will embed illustrations in the text as they write. However, that may cause problems. Image files are often several megabytes, which increases the book's file size. Instead of 500 KBs, you're suddenly dealing with 20 MBs. Most email programs won't let you send 20 MB files. Be sure to resize and compress the images.

There's another good reason to compress images. Part of Amazon's fee is based on your book's file size. If your file is unnecessarily large, your royalties will suffer. In your Word file, select an image and select Format | Pictures | Compress | All Pictures | Web Screen. This changes the images to 96 dpi. (Do this only for the version for the digital book; 96 dpi is too low for print.)

Tables don't show up well in digital devices (Kindle, iPads, smart phones, etc.). Fonts change and the layout becomes a mess. For the tables in this book, I created the tables in Word, zoomed in until the table filled the screen, made a screen grab, and saved the image. What you see is actually an image of a Word table. Save the original in PNG format but use a version in JPG (to reduce the file size).

Store the illustrations in a folder and add a reference in the text for the illustrator, along with a file name such as img-04-012.jpg (chapter 4, 12th image). The illustrator will generally need to edit the images, so the images should be in a folder.

Be sure to talk with the illustrator before you start making screenshots to make sure you're using the right image size and quality.

## Book Templates

You also need a book template. This is a word processor file that has all of the parts of the book so you only need to add your outline and text.

- If your book is for the mass market, you can use a simple template. You likely won't use footnotes, end notes, and other things. Layout can be a bit casual.

- When writing for academics or professionals, use a professional template. Your book should match the quality of books by major publishing houses. Serious book reviewers may note errors in the layout as evidence of amateur work.

Most publishers have free templates at their websites. You can use these, even if you publish elsewhere.

How to Write a Book! by Andreas Ramos

## RSI: The Pain of Writing

Despite movies of Jane Austen smiling softly as she scribbles, wri
can be painful. Any kind of writing, whether with a pen, typewrite
keyboard, can hurt your hands, wrists, and arms. This is *Repetitive
Stress Injury* (RSI), also known as writer's cramp or *carpal tunnel
syndrome*.

The name "writer's cramp" makes it sound like cramps in your legs
that go away in a few minutes. RSI can last day and night for six to
nine months. The pain can go away but a few days on a bad keyboard
can bring it back at full strength.

RSI is a common injury for writers. Many of our NWU writers had RSI.
I knew writers who weren't able to open a door or shake hands. At
night, your arms and hands feel swollen and throb in pain and you can
only sleep on your back.

Prevent RSI by using a good keyboard, an ergonomic keyboard tray,
wrist support, and an adjustable office chair with arm support. Take
every opportunity to get away from your desk. Every night after
dinner, we go for a 30-minute walk. On weekends, we often walk for
several hours.

If you have RSI, you must change your work station. Don't do things
that can hurt your hands. Vibrating tools, such as kitchen mixers or
electric drills, can aggravate RSI. Rest your arms and hands as much as
possible. Surgery treats the pain but not the cause of injury.

You can read more about RSI at http://goo.gl/CrAKYv

## An Office Chair

An office chair has adjustable arm rests to support your elbows. It
should also allow you to adjust the height. This helps to prevent RSI
injury.

Some people write on the sofa or in bed. Sure, you can do that, but
after a few years, you'll get RSI and you'll barely be able to lift a pencil.

Some people like to stand up when they write. I also know people who do this. I've asked them about this and they don't know if it's better or not. They prefer to stand.

For a low-cost solution, look for used office furniture stores.

## A Few Other Things

A few more things:

- You'll need a printer. I use a low-cost inkjet printer. You can print in draft mode (fast print) so it prints faster and saves ink. You can buy inexpensive ink refill kits at any office supply store. There are also inexpensive laser printers.

- Most people use the computer mouse to select a menu item, place the cursor in the text, drag to select text, and so on. That's a problem because your fingers leave the keyboard, which slows you down. Instead, you should learn to use accelerator keys, such as *Control + C* to copy and *Control + V* to insert. There are accelerator keys for search, replace, repeat search, select a column in a table, select a row, print, and more. You can create accelerator keys to select the entire sentence, select to the end of the sentence, or select a paragraph. You'll be able to write faster.

- You'll also need pens in red or blue to mark up your text. I edit on paper, so I make changes in blue or red. Don't use black; it's hard to see your changes on a printout.

- A whiteboard is also useful for discussing ideas in meetings. You can buy a six-foot (2m) whiteboard for about $100. Better yet, you can buy a whiteboard paint that turns any wall into a whiteboard. It's about $25 for a bucket at any large hardware store. Paint the wall and you'll have a huge whiteboard. You can use dry-erase marker pens (whiteboard pens). To clean it, use whiteboard spray cleaner. You can also mix one part isopropyl alcohol (plain rubbing alcohol) with three parts water in a spray bottle.

How to Write a Book! by Andreas Ramos

## Your Daily Backups

You must make daily backups. Backups must be safe from theft or fire.

You can use a calendar date in the backup file name, such as Book-0314 (March 14th). Every time you edit, save with today's date.

- Don't use memory chips: they can get lost, be stolen, or the cat knocks it under the desk.

- Don't use external backup disk drives. These drives can lose data. They can also be stolen.

- Don't store backup in your house or office. Buildings can burn down.

The easiest and safest solution is a free online storage site. A better solution is to synchronize your hard disk to the online storage service. This means your files are constantly backed up.

These storage sites are replicated in several cities, so when Chicago celebrates by burning down the city, your file will be safe on duplicate sites in Dallas and Denver. Every night, I drag a copy of the book file into a web-based storage site. You can use Box.com, Dropbox, Google Drive, Microsoft OneDrive, or whatever you like.

When Hemingway was starting out as a writer, an editor heard of him and asked to see more of his writing. Hemingway's wife packed up all of his writings, including originals, copies, and carbon copies, in a suitcase and set off from Paris to Switzerland. At the train station, she went to get a bottle of water. Somebody stole the suitcase.

## After the Writing Is Done

After you've finished the book, store the final book file, along with signed permissions from people, interviews, research notes, and unused material. This lets you reuse your work years later.

## Summary of this Chapter

Your writing tools are an expense which you can deduct from taxes. Keep receipts and talk with your tax accountant.

# The Author Speaks: Eva Maria Knudsen

Eva Maria Knudsen wrote *Co-Parenting in Divorced Families* (2011), which was self published in Denmark. Eva's website is 2hjem.dk

## Why Do You Write?

Because I think I have something to contribute. Also I have something I can give away for free. It's nice to give something to other people.

## How Has Writing Affected Your Life and Career?

It hasn't yet. But I learned I can write and I actually had something worthwhile to say.

## Do You Prefer Self Publishing or Traditional?

I published my book as a PDF and distributed it via website and newsletter.

## What's Your Experience with Self Publishing?

I would recommend everybody to have a professional editor for both quality and grammar. That makes you less doubtful about the quality of your book and it enhances the quality.

## What Would You Have Done Differently?

I should have published short sections of the book on my website, in a blog, etc. And I should have cooperated with others to add their comments to the book. I should also have made a deal with a company that would offer the book to their customers. My biggest challenge was to design the book and know what kind of publishing tools I should have used.

# 9. Legal Stuff about Writing

## Introduction

This chapter covers legal issues about your book. This isn't legal advice. I'm not a lawyer. Don't ask for my lawyer. You can talk with my cat but he won't reply. He's a cat.

## How Do I Copyright my Book?

You automatically have a copyright when you write something in the US. You don't need to use the copyright symbol or register.

To notify ownership of your work, use a copyright statement after the title. For example, "*The Catcher in the Rye* © 1951 by J. D. Salinger, USA."

You can also place a copyright notice at the front of your book. For example: "*The Catcher in the Rye* © 1951 by J. D. Salinger, USA. All rights reserved. This document is protected by copyright. No part of this document may be reproduced in any form by any means without prior written permission from the author."

You can register your copyright at the US Copyright Office (copyright.gov) with a small fee. Their FAQ has an overview of the benefits of copyright.

If you register the copyright, you get additional legal privileges, such as statutory damages and the right to collect legal fees. This means that you can collect the royalty, additional penalties, and legal expenses.

However… it's very expensive to do anything about copyright. Copyright law is federal law, so you'll need a lawyer who can appear in federal court. If someone steals your book, it may cost you $25,000 to $50,000 just to hire your lawyer. If someone turns your book into a movie where you're played by Tom Cruise, there's enough money so you can sue and get money. But if it's a YouTube video where you're played by a cat, forget it. For the vast majority of copyright violations, you're legally right but sadly, there's nothing you can do about it.

- If you self publish, then you decide if you want to register the copyright (and pay the fee).

- If a publisher prints the book, then the publisher holds the copyright so the publisher will register (and pay the fee).

## How Do I Get a Copyright in My Country?

Copyright laws are different in every country. Contact writers' organizations in your country and see if they can offer advice.

## Can I Write Anonymously? What about Copyright?

Some people don't want to use their name. They may not like their name or they think their name isn't good for the public. Some people want to publish anonymously, so they use a pseudonym. Many publishers accept this and allow pseudonyms.

The US Copyright Office however requires a real name. If you still want to remain anonymous, you can register the book under someone else's name (a friend, etc.).

Of course, a pseudonym goes against the point of this book. If you publish under a pseudonym, it's not going to help your career or reputation. Nobody will know you were the author.

## What about Liability?

Many people ask me about liability, as if they're afraid they'll be sued for saying something. In general, this isn't an issue. Most companies are happy if you write about them because it's free publicity (okay, not if you're writing about their bad business activities). If you're writing an expose, be sure to document and prove what you say.

How to Write a Book! by Andreas Ramos

## Plagiary and Other People's Text

When someone copies from another person's book, it's called plagiarism. The doctrine of fair use allows you to copy text. But there are gray areas. There are also times where there's no right to copy. For example, you can't copy a single line from music lyrics. There have been numerous lawsuits, settlements, and court decisions over this.

Be careful with gray areas. If there's doubt, talk with your publisher.

Plagiary may lead to public ridicule for the writer. A number of politicians and celebrities have been caught at copying other people's work. In Germany, both Karl-Theodor zu Guttenberg, minister of defense, and Annette Scharan, minister of education, plagiarized their dissertations and were forced to resign.

It's easy these days to check for plagiary. Many universities use software to see if the students have copied text from websites. Some publishers also check for plagiary. You can also use these tools to see if others have copied your work.

## What Can You Do if Your Work Is Pirated?

On the one hand, it's flattering. Wow, your book is good enough that people want to steal it. On the other hand, it's dismaying. They're selling your book and you get nothing. And it undercuts your publisher's sales as well. One of these sites sold 50,000 copies of my books. I got nothing.

What can you do about? When I saw my books were being distributed by a pirate site, I talked with my publisher. They knew about the site and several more. But the websites are scam operations and if you sue, they just shut down and open up under a different name. So there's nothing you can do about it.

### Do I Need Permission to write a review?

You can review whatever you like. Write a fair review and compare the product with leading similar products. Don't just describe the features. Write from your experience and say whether it's useful or not.

If you specialize in a field and you review many products in that field, you may get free products from the manufacturers. For many years, I wrote a monthly magazine column where I often reviewed products. Marketing teams added my name to their reviewer list and every few days, the post office delivered boxes of samples to my door. You can keep the stuff. But what can you do with 28 computer mice? To get on lists like this, send copies of your published reviews to the head of marketing at companies.

### Can I Use Someone Else's Literary Character?

If the copyright has expired, the book goes into the public domain, which means everyone owns it, including you. You can publish (and sell) the book, use the characters in your own book, write sequels to the book, make T-shirts, and keep the money.

In some cases, it can be difficult to decide who owns the copyright. Disney pretends to own the rights to the Little Mermaid, which was written by Hans Christian Andersen in Denmark in1837, so the copyright expired decades ago. But who can afford to argue with Disney's 400 lawyers?

### Can I Copy from Wikipedia?

If you include the source and you give it away, yes, you can copy Wikipedia. But you can't sell it. And you can't present it as your work. That violates the Wikipedia copyright. Be careful with Wikipedia. Because it's a volunteer project, it's often inaccurate.

### Summary of this Chapter

I cover only a few common legal issues that may affect nonfiction writers. In general, you won't have legal problems.

# The Author Speaks: Gillian Bagwell

Gillian Bagwell is the author of three historical novels. *The Darling Strumpet*, based on the life of Nell Gwynn, seventeenth-century actress and mistress of Charles II, was a finalist for a Romance Writers of America RITA award for Best First Book. Her second book, *The September Queen*, was the first fictional accounting of the extraordinary adventure of Jane Lane, who risked her life to help the young Charles II escape after the disastrous Battle of Worcester. *Venus in Winter*, published in July 2013, is based on the first forty years of the life of the formidable four-times widowed Tudor dynast.

Gillian began her professional life in theatre, first as an actress and later as a director and producer. She founded the Pasadena Shakespeare Company and ran it for nine years, producing thirty-seven successful productions and directing nine of them, and she now puts her theatre background to use by coaching writers on giving effective public readings. She also offers all levels of editing, specializing in historical fiction and romance. Gillian lives in Berkeley, California, and is at work on her fourth novel. Visit Gillian at GillianBagwell.com.

## How Long Have You Been Writing?

I've been writing here and there all my life, but didn't make it my professional focus until 2005, when I was living in London to care for my dying mother. Before that, I didn't have a focus for my creative energy.

## Why Do You Write?

I think I write because I love to read and at some level I'm probably writing the books I'd like to read if someone else had written them!

## How Has Writing Affected Your Life and Career?

I began writing my first novel when I had to put my personal and professional life on hold and everything was up in the air. When I went back home to California from London, I decided to finish my book and sell it. I did and my life changed completely.

### How Did You Find and Choose Your Publisher?

I was fortunate to have an agent interested in me before I had a complete first draft of my first novel, so she and her foreign rights agent and associated agent in the UK have taken care of selling my books to publishers. These days, many novelists, especially writers of romance, opt to self publish, but being published by one of the major publishers still gives advantages that self publishing doesn't, and the only way to get a contract with a major publishing house is through an agent.

### Did It Help to Have a Lawyer Review Your Contract?

I've only worked with agents, not lawyers, for my contracts.

### What's the Best Way to Promote Your Book?

I've done blog tours, which means guest posts, giveaways, and reviews on several book blogs, especially those related to historical fiction. This has gotten the word out about my books and helped me find readers who love historical fiction. I've also done bookstore readings in Pasadena, Berkeley, and Corte Madera for my books.

I'm fairly active on Twitter and Facebook, posting about writing, history, and language that I think my readers will find interesting.

I'm active in the Historical Novel Society and have spoken on panels at the annual conferences both in the US and UK. I also periodically teach workshops on writing historical fiction and on giving effective public readings. I've also spoken alone or with other authors at libraries and other venues. I think all of this helps keep my books and me in front of people who'll enjoy them.

### What Would You Have Done Differently?

I don't know that I would have done anything differently. I've been very lucky.

# 10. Publishing Your Book

## *Introduction*

Okay, so you have a manuscript. Now you want to get it published. There are two ways: find a publisher or publish it yourself. There are advantages and drawbacks to each of these.

## *Should you Self-Publish or Find a Publisher?*

There are several ways to publish your book:

- **Self-published Author**: You write the book and also manage editing, layout, distribution, and marketing. You can distribute digital books or printed via Kindle, Lulu, Smashwords, Nook, and Amazon. You can also distribute PDF by email, on a blog or a website.

- **Independent Publisher**: These are small specialized publishing houses. They specialize in genre fiction (such as detective or science fiction), business topics, or academic publishing, generally led by people who love books. You write the book and the independent publisher does the editing, layout, printing, marketing, and distribution in digital, paperback, and hardback. You get a royalty.

- **Big House Publishers**: The big publishing houses may employ thousands of people and have offices worldwide. These include Random House, McGraw-Hill, and IDG. Just like independent publishing, the big house publishers take care of editing, layout, printing, distribution, and marketing. You get a royalty.

- **Vanity Press**: These printing companies pretend to be publishers. You send your manuscript and several thousand dollars and they print it for you. You get a few hundred printed books with your name on it. These printers take advantage of the author's desperation to be published.

The distinctions overlap and it depends on who's talking. Smashwords and Lulu use the phrase "independent publishing" and "indie publishing" to cover writers who publish their own work. Some talk about small publishers and large publishers.

The difference between independent publishing and big-house publishing is like independent film studios (indie films) and Hollywood film studios. Just as indie film makers specialize in documentaries or special movies, independent publishers also specialize in niche fields.

The author's experience depends on the publisher. Independent publishers collaborate with the author like a coach and shares knowledge and experience. The publisher is also more flexible with the content, the process, and the deadlines. With a big-house publisher, there's less personal attention. The author is expected to know how to write and deliver the manuscript. The text is held to a higher standard.

In either case, you have to collaborate with your publisher. You can't just write a text and toss it over the fence. Publishers are working dozens or hundreds of other writers. The more you work with your publisher, the more attention you'll get.

If we look only at the results (the printed book), there isn't much difference. Technology allows anyone now to produce books at the same quality as large publishers and use Amazon to distribute worldwide.

The difference is in the selection and editing process. Publishers select the writers. Publishers, both small independents or big names, give guidance and feedback. The books go through content review and editing for grammar and style. For academic or scholarly books, the publisher's editorial contribution is critical to ensure the book meets the high standard of quality for academia.

## *So, What's Better? Self-Publish or Big Publisher?*

So how should you publish your books? There isn't a clear answer.

- If you self publish, you have control over the production, profits, distribution, and marketing. You can use the book in many different ways for marketing and promotion. You can reuse your text for other books and formats. You can release each chapter as a separate ebook. You can give it away. You keep control over your text. If IBM wants to give a chapter of your book to their 400,000 employees, it's up to you. If you gave the publishing rights to a publisher, the publisher makes the decision, which can take months to happen. The downside of self publishing is extra time and work.

- If you work with an independent publisher, you'll have a partner who has deep experience in your subject and profession. That can develop into a long-term relationship.

- If your book is published by a big publisher, you'll get the cachet and name recognition of a large brand. To be published by McGraw-Hill, IDG, Wiley, or similar is a mark of excellence.

Whatever you choose, one thing is common: you must do the marketing yourself. You must develop a long-term strategy of writing books for your career by using marketing and promotion that includes a website, an email newsletter, digital advertising, speaking events, and more.

Don't worry about the East Coast obsession with big publishers. People on the East Coast, especially in Manhattan, think they're a real writer only if they're published by one of the large publishers. However, the astonishing success of *50 Shades of Grey* and other self-published books changed the industry.

## Printed Book or an eBook?

There are many ways to release a book:

- **PDF**: The easy solution is Adobe PDF. You write the book and save it as a PDF file, which you can share via email or on a webpage. Just about every digital device can display PDF. If you want to make a correction or update a section, just save a new PDF. It's a quick and simple solution. I use PDF for my ebooks at Andreas.com. There are other formats but PDF is easy to create, works everywhere, and it's free.

- **HTML**: Many tools let you convert a text file into an HTML file for the web.

- **Digital books and eBooks**. Digital books (ebooks)can be read on tablets such as Kindle, iPad, Nook, and Kobo plus smart phones. When you upload your book to Amazon or Smashwords, your file is converted into an ebook format for digital readers.

- **Printed books by POD**: Printing can now be done by Print on Demand (POD) machines. It's a book robot about the size of a refrigerator. You select the file and it creates the printed book in about ten minutes. Instead of printing (and storing) 1,500 books, POD book robots print one at a time. You can print what you need. POD can produce hardback or paperback. Amazon CreateSpace and similar services use POD. Paperback POD books can be less than $3 each.

- **Printed books by publishers**. The large publishers use an industrial printing press to produce a book. These machines can be as large as a locomotive and require teams of specialists. The paper rolls weigh several tons. The books are hardback (cloth) or paperback. Big house publishers, such as McGraw-Hill or Wiley, pay attention to quality and details, so their books generally have excellent layout, copyediting, illustrations, front material, glossary, and indexing.

How to Write a Book! by Andreas Ramos

### Should You Print Books? Or Is Digital Good Enough?

Although digital books get lots of attention at the moment, it's much better for your professional recognition when you hand someone a printed book.

Among professional writers, we often say a book is a "one-pound business card." People love to get a book from an author because there are so few authors. They really like a personally-autographed book. They put that on their desk; they remember the author. Okay, most likely, they won't read it, but they'll appreciate it. And when they need your skill, they'll remember you.

A printed book has something that digital formats don't have: a book has *thunk*. That's the *"thunk!"* when you drop it on a desk. It's physical. PDFs and blogs don't have that. Magazine articles are thrown away. But books are real.

Books also work better at a book signing event, a conference, or a tradeshow. People prefer to get a printed book.

As the author, you can buy books from your publisher at about 50% discount from the cover price or, if you publish via Amazon, you can buy from Amazon at a very low cost (I pay $2.77 for my books). I bought cases of books and gave copies to prospects and clients. We got several large clients because they found the books in bookstores.

Another tip: keep books nearby. I have a box of books at the office and another box in the trunk of my car so I can give books to people.

### One Book? Or a Series? Monographs versus Serialization

If you ask a professor what she's working on, she'll reply she's writing a monograph. That's the academic way of saying that she's writing a book. A monograph is a book on a single topic, such as archaeology in Peru.

To professors and most literary writers, books are written as stand-alone items. My previous books were monographs. Some of the books had websites, but there wasn't a connection between the books.

You should write books as part of a series. The various books should cover different aspects of your field. This lets you build an audience and your reputation. You also build connections within your industry as you interview experts, meet other authors, speak at events, and similar.

By the way, don't make a website for each book. Many authors make websites for each book but after six months, the author goes on to other projects and those sites are abandoned. Many of your visitors will go to those abandoned sites. It's better to bring your visitors to one site where they can see all of your books, both past and current. Create your author's site and put all of your books at your site.

## What about a Book Agent?

Also called a literary agent, a book agent has experience with the publishing process, such as the contract, the fees, and the marketing. Your agent also knows what's realistic in terms of royalties and advances. He can guide you and help you at every step. Agents get 10-15% of your royalties.

An agent's value is in the sale of additional rights, such as film rights. If you write fiction and it can be made into a movie, an agent can get this done. Book publishers know how to publish books; they don't make movies. So you'll need someone who can navigate the world of movie studios.

If your books are selling hundreds of thousands of copies and there's a chance it can be a movie, then yes, talk with an agent who knows how to do this.

But that's not likely for most nonfiction books. As you'll notice in the interviews, none of the authors work with agents.

## How Do You Get a Book Agent?

There are several ways to get an agent:

- Build a track record in publishing. That means you've published several books with traditional publishers and you have verified book sales. Agents will call you.

- Become a best-selling self-published author at Amazon. Write a book, sell 50,000 copies at Amazon, and agents will call you. All of the top authors at Amazon are called by agents.

- Get an author with an agent to recommend you to his agent. If the author thinks you can write, he may talk with his agent and the agent may call you.

- Be a celebrity, sports star, CEO, or national politician. Agents will call you. Or ask your PR team to call an agent.

If you don't have any of this, it's unlikely an agent will talk with you. It's hard enough to get a publisher to consider your manuscript; it's the same with agents. They only work with authors who make money for them.

Make sure the agent can deliver. If you get all happy that you've gotten an agent but two years go by and nothing happens, that's two years wasted where you could have had a better agent. Talk with the agent's other authors. Talk with the agent's publishing houses. Make sure the agent is currently active. You won't get much from an agent who got a book published ten years ago. The publishing industry constantly changes and if they don't have current connections, it won't matter.

In general, you'll do just as well if you go directly to the publisher, plus you keep the money. For most non-fiction authors, there's little advantage in working with an agent.

With the rise of self publishing, there isn't much need for a book agent. You can easily get your book into Amazon. If it sells well, publishers will see it and contact you directly. If it doesn't sell, an agent isn't going to make a difference.

Be careful with what some writers say about agents. Some writers are convinced their agent is stopping them from big sales and the Nobel Prize. So you may see strong opinions against book agents.

## They Really Are Against You

And there's a bit of truth to that. Doris Lessing wrote two dozen novels and got every literary prize, including the Nobel. In the early 1980s, she wanted to show that many writers were right: they weren't being published because they weren't famous. So she signed her manuscript as "Jane Somers" and sent it to her agents, publishers, and reviewers. Every one rejected it. The book was published under that name and sold poorly. One reviewer even dismissed it as "not very good Lessing."

It's the paradox of writing: many people read your books only if many people read your books. It's hard to climb out of the pit of obscurity.

## The Next Step: Hybrid Book Agents

A number of book agents have realized they know enough about publishing to do it themselves. They know the authors, they're familiar with the process of editing and layout, and they can use Amazon or Smashwords to produce books. So some book agents have set up their own publishing houses.

They find authors who were previously published but can't get a publisher for the next book. Or they find authors who have books that the publishers aren't promoting anymore.

This is similar to groups of authors who set up their own imprints. Some of these groups are exclusive: you must have previously been published by established, reputable publishing houses.

## So Digital Books Are the Future? Remember DTP?

We've been here before. In the late 1980s, publishing went through a technological revolution. Until then, layout involved typesetting, which was complex and expensive. The new desktop publishing (DTP) software on Apple Macintosh in the US and Atari ST in Europe let you do layout for books and magazines. Thousands of small shops began to publish magazines and books even though they didn't know anything about book production or layout. The results were mostly amateurish.

DTP died in 1993 when multimedia introduced interactive design that combined text, images, video, and music on a CD or DVD disk. Music, voice, and video made it more appealing than printed paper.

Two years later, in 1995, the web took off. It wasn't limited to disks. DTP and multimedia were quickly forgotten as everyone began to create websites.

So it may look today like Amazon is going to take over the world, but as you can see, this has happened before. So what's next?

Although much of the last thirty years has revolved around the technological developments in publishing, I think that's coming to an end. Production and distribution is now both very good and very cheap. On the downside, these tools allow many people to publish junk. I think the next phase in publishing will be over quality. The junk writers will occupy the bargain bins at Amazon and Walmart. Serious writers and publishers will offer professional books. Publishers will develop their brand recognition as a seal of quality.

## *Summary of this Chapter*

Publish or self publish? Print or digital? Domestic or imported? It was much easier for Hemingway. He sent in his manuscripts and if anyone didn't like it, he punched them in the nose. Today, things are evolving rapidly. Whatever you choose, you'll probably do it differently in few years, so take a best-for-now approach.

# The Author Speaks: Bruce Hartford

Bruce Hartford lives in San Francisco. He's working on *The Selma Voting Rights Struggle and the March to Montgomery* (forthcoming) and *Mississippi Freedom Summer 1964* (forthcoming). He wrote *The Gandhi Ring* (Westwind Writers, 2006). He has been writing in one genre or another since 1970. Visit him at CRMVet.org.

## Why Do You Write?

To communicate and advocate.

## How Has Writing Affected Your Life and Career?

Writing has been my career.

## Do You Prefer Self Publishing or Traditional?

In theory, I'd prefer traditional publisher, but what I write isn't likely to be traditionally published, so I don't waste my time looking for that.

## How Did You Find and Choose Your Publisher?

I've always self published my books.

## What's Your Experience with Self Publishing?

The bad side is the low access to my audience and markets. I've have to do all of the promotion work on my own. There's a lack of ways to economically promote my work, both in terms of time and money.

## Do You Have an Agent?

No, I've never needed that.

## What's the Best Way to Promote Your Book?

In my case, I sent emails to contacts. I also spoke at many events and conferences.

## What Would You Have Done Differently?

I should have been born into a rich family!

# 11. Self-Publishing Your Book

## Introduction

As I said, this book covers how to write books to enhance your career. In the chapters on how to self publish your book, I cover only Amazon because I choose to keep it simple for my purposes. There are many other options and paths for self publishing, printing, sales, and distribution. The best overview of self publishing is in Carla King's books *Self-Publishing Boot Camp* and *How to Self-Publish Your Book*.

The following is my experience with self publishing, what works for me, and how to use it for yourself to get your books to your readers.

## Why Self-Publish?

My first eight books were printed by traditional publishers, including McGraw-Hill, Tsinghua University Press, and Jain Press. While I was researching for my ninth book, I had lunch with Janus Boye in Denmark, who runs a major technology conference in the USA and Denmark. I asked him if it was really worthwhile to give away books for free instead of selling them. He said yes, in his experience, free worked better than paid for nonfiction books because it increased the reach to his audience and that's what mattered. The more people who know you, the more will contact you.

So I gambled on this with *The Big Book of Content Marketing*. I had a publisher for the book, but I wrote to him and said I'd release the book myself on Amazon. Yes, I turned down a publisher.

Normally, I write the text, hand the file over to the publisher, and they take care of the rest. Now I had to do it all myself.

Because I had control over the distribution, I could reach a wider audience. I did three or four webinars for large companies. Some of these companies had more than 10,000 people on their mailing list, so I let the companies offer the book as a PDF. People also downloaded the book from my website. The book was available at conferences and events. Some 50,000 copies were distributed.

## Book Production Services: Digital and Print

There are a number of book production services, including Amazon, Smashwords, and Lulu. These produce both digital and print books.

You can look into these and compare the service, costs, features, and audience size. I use Amazon because it works and it's easy.

Amazon offers two services, one for digital books and the other for print books:

- Amazon Kindle Direct Publishing (KDP) produces digital books (ebooks). These can be read on Amazon Kindle tablets, Apple iPads, all tablets, and all smart phones. With free Kindle software, Kindle books can also be read on all laptop and desktop computers.
- Amazon CreateSpace produces printed books in paperback or hardback.

There's also Amazon Author Central, which is your author's page at Amazon. You add your photo, bio, and a list of books. Be sure to fill out your page at Amazon Author Central

## Don't Use a Vanity Press

In desperation to get published, some authors pay printing companies to print their book. These printing companies are called vanity presses.

What's the difference between traditional publishing, self publishing via Amazon, and a vanity press?

- Traditional publishers and Amazon publishing make money by selling books to people. If nobody reads it, they don't make money.

- Vanity presses make money by selling books to the author. The vanity press doesn't care if nobody reads it.

Vanity presses take advantage of the author's desire to be published. Authors see publishers as a stamp of approval. However, approval comes from the readers, not the publisher.

You see ads for vanity presses in many magazines. These companies charge high fees to produce the book. They also add additional fees for marketing or publicity services.

Stay away from vanity presses such as AuthorHouse, Author Solutions, BookTango, iUniverse, Palibrio, Trafford, and Xlibris.

I've met people who paid $5,000 to get 100 copies of their book so they could distribute these to colleagues. That's $50 per book (and they first had to pay $5,000).

It's free to print your book at Amazon, Smashwords, or similar services. You buy the books for less than $3 per book. You can also do much better publicity on your own for less money.

## How Do I Set the Price?

You set your book's sales price at Amazon. You can set it to whatever you like.

Mark Coker, founder of Smashwords, looked at sales data for tens of thousands of books and found in general, books at $2.99 sell 6.2 times more copies than books over $10. That also means you'll earn more at $2.99 than at $10 (for details, see http://goo.gl/clwxHB).

Let's say you sell 1,000 books at $10. That's $10,000 in sales. If we assume Smashwords' 6.2X multiple and you price it at $2.99, you may sell 6,200 books, which is $18,538. You make more with a lower price, plus you get six times as many readers.

## How Much Royalties Will I Get from Amazon?

You can get up to 70% of the US sales price for an ebook at Amazon. Yes, seventy percent. Stephen King gets only 25% from his publisher.

The amount from Amazon ranges from 35% to 70%, depending on the country and the sales price.

In contrast, publishers give you an advance on the expected royalties. Amazon pays only if there are sales. However, you get a higher royalty. Amazon keeps the remainder to cover its costs. The customer pays the shipping fees.

You don't pay Amazon CreateSpace. There are no setup fees or printing costs for you. You upload your book, set the price, and sit back. If it sells, you get a share of the selling price. If it doesn't sell, there's no cost to you.

## Buying Your Books from Amazon?

You can buy your books from Amazon. They charge for printing and shipping. I pay $2.77 for my printed books. You can buy as many or as few as you like (yes, even one at a time).

## Can I Make Money by Self-Publishing?

Here's some data on writers' income in 2013:

- 1.8% of self-published authors earned over $100,000

- 8.8% of traditionally published authors earned over $100,000

- 13.2% of hybrid authors (published as both self-published and traditionally-published) earned over $100,000

- 60% of indie authors earn less than $5,000

Data from a study by Dana Beth Weinberg, Ph.D., professor of sociology at Queens College in NYC and reported in Forbes at http://goo.gl/zCgwNw.

This means most authors don't make a living from their books. Some authors like to write. Some authors write as part of their career (that's what I do). How much you make will depend on how well you promote your books.

## Problems with Printing at Amazon

In general, the printing process at Amazon is smooth. We had trouble with the cover. First, the cover was designed in Paris, so the text on the spine was in the European style. The base of a US book spine points toward the back cover; a European book spine points to the front cover. This means if you look at a bookcase of European books, you lean your head to the left; if it's American, you lean to the right. So we made a European and an American cover.

We then ran into another cover problem. For some reason, Amazon's computer rejected our cover. We spent two months trying different sizes and file formats. We never found out why this was happening. In the end, I talked with Amazon and paid $100 for them to adjust the cover.

## You Can Print Just One Book to See How It Looks

POD lets you print one book at a time. You finish your layout, upload the book, and then buy one copy of your printed book to see how it looks in print. You can make changes and try again.

If you want to see the quality of Word and Amazon publishing, buy a copy of my content marketing book and compare it with books by major publishers. It's the same production quality.

## What's My Rank at Amazon?

Don't worry about your Amazon Author Rank (reported in your account at Amazon Author Central). If your book is in the top 10,000, that's good. If it's below that, it doesn't really matter. It's logarithmic, so rank can fluctuate wildly from day to day. Ask a mathematician to explain this. Or don't worry about it.

## Can I Publish My Collection of Poems?

On a side note, several people asked me if they could use this to publish personal work, such as their poems, or family history. Yes, that's a great way to do this. If it's personal, you don't have to bother with copyrights, ISBN, or an index. Just use a template, drop the text in, adjust the layout, and print at Amazon. You can produce books for less than $3 each. You can make as many or as few as you want.

## Summary of this Chapter

I write books to advance my career, so I use a quick and easy solution. However, there are many ways to produce, sell, and distribute books. You can look into those to find better ways to do this.

# The Author Speaks: Carla King

Carla King is an adventure travel journalist whose accounts of solo journeys around the world are published widely online and in print. She has self published since 1994, and in 2010 she co-founded the Self-Publishing Boot Camp program of books and seminars. She's written seven books including her *Motorcycle Misadventures Series* and *Stories from Elsewhere* travel anthology, plus her *Self-Publishing Boot Camp Guide for Authors*. Her travel writing has been included in many anthologies including Best Travel Writing 2011, and her self-publishing advice is published widely online. Carla's first writing, a haiku, was published by her second-grade teacher Miss Anderson. Carla lives in San Diego. Wherever she is, you can find her at CarlaKing.com.

## Why Do You Write?

I write to share my observations about the world around me, to remember, forget, share, and work out how things are.

## How Has Writing Affected Your Life and Career?

Writing has everything to do with my life and career. My first temp job typing out handwritten user guides turned into a technical writing career because I'd automatically correct and improve the writing. I also put together little how-to tips about the new word processing systems for the secretaries and writers. When the tech writing manager needed someone new on her staff, she hired me. I hadn't even finished my second year of college. Later, after my first trip overseas, I attended a travel writing conference to learn what editors want. There, I met Allen Noren who had ridden his BMW motorcycle to the conference. We talked in the parking lot where I found out that he ran O'Reilly's Global Network Navigator website (later sold to AOL). He needed writers who knew enough about tech to FTP stories from afar. After I told him about my upcoming job test riding a Russian motorcycle on behalf of the American importers, I was hired. My journey around the USA on the Russian motorcycle became the *American Borders Motorcycle Diaries*, sent to the web in real time from the road and my first paid travel writing gig. At first I was shocked to get feedback from readers in real time via email, but soon I was addicted. Finally, I knew what readers wanted! After that, I split my time between travel writing, which didn't pay much, and my highly-paid gigs as managing editor for websites and internal magazines for the likes of Sun Microsystems and Sony PlayStation, which I also enjoyed. Today I split my time between travel writing and teaching and writing for Self-Pub Boot Camp.

## Do You Prefer Self Publishing or Traditional?

I self published from the start because I'd already written so many tech manuals that the process didn't daunt me. In 1993 I wrote a little guide to bicycling the French Riviera that was rejected by a traditional publisher, who liked it but wanted a "bigger" book. So I simply did it on my own, hiring a graphic artist to draw maps, and a cover designer. I flew back to Nice with a couple of boxes of books, hired a car and sold it to English-language bookstores, bicycle shops, and tourist offices. I made enough money to fund two more trips. *Cycling the French Riviera* is out of print but still a great little book I keep meaning to sell as an ebook.

My only experience with traditional publishing was with my writing group the Wild Writing Women who self published our *Stories of World Travel* anthology in 2000. It was wildly successful, selling out in a week. Some of us went to Book Expo America in New York to promote the book to booksellers by handing out postcards, and honestly, just to see what BEA was all about. It was exciting! As early self publishers, we didn't get much interest from booksellers but we got an astounding 18 letters of interest from traditional publishers. I didn't want a publisher, but our group of 12 voted 7-to-5 to hand it to Globe-Pequot because they had the best marketing plan. Unfortunately, Globe barely promoted it and we haven't seen a penny in royalties to this day.

## What's the Best Way to Promote Your Book?

I've found the techniques used to promote my travel writing and my self-publishing how-to guides are very different. The people who buy my travel books like to interact with me in person. I go to the big motorcycle shows, where I get a booth in exchange for a few talks over the weekend, and people literally throw twenty dollar bills on my table all day long. My hand cramps from signing so many books, especially before the holidays because expo-attendees are flush and looking for gifts. Much of my audience is also very very active in social media and forums, where they appreciate advice about what motorcycle to ride in what destination, how to pack, what gear to wear, what tools to bring. This is true for any niche area in adventure travel, not only motorcycles, but 4x4s, paddle boarding, and scuba diving. Themes like solo women's travel are also high-touch in social media. They like to know me and so the more I reply "in-person" to greetings on Facebook, Twitter, and email, the more books I sell.

I don't have to promote myself as an expert in adventure travel because the trips I've done speak for themselves and my prominent presence on the web make it obvious. In self publishing that isn't the case. Though I was self publishing early - only Dan Poynter entered the field earlier than I did! - today the market is very crowded and every author who's made a book with CreateSpace gives free talks and writes well-meaning but often misguided blog posts about it. In this environment it's difficult to get people to pay for a book or a workshop. But authors eventually do get to me... the trick, I think - and I still haven't figured all of this out - is to simply plod along as the most reliable source of information out there. To keep testing products and services, write about them honestly, give away a lot of free information, and generally, rise above. Blogging works, but lately I've noticed that audio and video podcasts work well, especially interviews. When other experts in the field trust me, then my audience does, too. This is why it's important to cultivate not potential audience and your influencers.

## What Would You Have Done Differently?

Looking back, I think I would have published many more small books or booklets instead of caching away material for larger works. I would have delivered these materials on the web and in print. I'd also have tried to conform a bit more to the kind of writing that magazines wanted in order to gain name recognition. That is, writing a piece that promoted a popular destination - like Hawaii, whose tourist board has an advertising budget - rather than a place like Guinea Bissau which of course is a thousand times more interesting but won't pay. And I'd have taken a lot more photos and done more filming, even though I'm lousy at it.

For my writing and expertise in self publishing, I believe I should have partnered early with an association such as IBPA to gain more recognition and to gain access to the publishing information available only to the inner circle. My association with PBS Mediashift does that for me now. I get early access to beta products, announced only to influencers.

I don't believe I'd have ever been happy with traditional publishing. I'm a loner by nature and I like the control that self publishing gives me. I'm not afraid of technology and enjoy learning how to do things myself. I appreciate my years in hi-tech because it gave me experience with tools like InDesign, HTML, WIKI markup, audio and video editing tools, version control systems, and project management, not to mention the experience of leading teams. I love working with engineering, production, and design people. It appeals to my writerly curiosity and observant nature to enter each world to learn a bit about it. But most of all I'm simply addicted to the freedom the new tools and the web provides. Traditional publishing hasn't caught up to the flexibility that the new tech gives authors, even though they're trying. There are lots of great new technology-driven hybrid publishing enterprises jumping in to fill the gaps and employ all of those out-of-work employees from the failed traditional publishing empire. I think it's fascinating and fabulous and a huge opportunity for authors, most of whom unfortunately remain rather timid about embarking on the self-publishing adventure.

# 12. Get a Traditional Publisher

## Introduction

The other way to produce your book is to have it published by a publisher. In this chapter, we'll look at how publishers choose manuscripts, produce books, and sell books. This also includes what a publisher can do for you and what it means to have a publisher.

## How Do I Find a Publisher?

There are several ways to find publishers:

- You can look for publishers. The best way to do this is with *The Writer's Market*, by Robert Brewer, which is updated yearly. It lists thousands of publishers and what they want to publish. You should also look at *Books in Print*. Both are in most libraries.

- If you've written books for a publisher, he likes working with you, and he notices an opportunity in a new market, he'll ask you write another book.

- If your books have done well, another publisher may ask you to write for them. Several publishers have asked me for books.

- You can also ask someone who's been published to refer you to her publisher. This puts you in touch through trusted connections. A friend wanted to publish her book and I referred her to a major publisher, who published her book. So this really happens (don't send me your book proposals!)

How to Write a Book! by Andreas Ramos

Here's another way. In the mid-2000s, I wanted the my next book to be available in bookstores, so I went to the large bookstores (*Borders* and *Barnes & Nobles*), found the section for computer books, and wrote down the names of the publishers. These publishers were big enough to be able to place books in large bookstores. I then went to each publisher's website and looked at their catalog to see if they had a book on my topic. Of 20-30 publishers, six didn't have a book on SEO. So I wrote to them. Two offered to publish the book.

## Why Is It Useful to Have a Book Publisher?

There are several advantages to working with a large publisher.

First, writers benefit from the publisher's brand recognition. To be published by a large publisher is a strong professional credential. In a specialist topic, only a handful of authors are published by the major publishers.

Because two of my books were published by McGraw-Hill, I was introduced to Tsinghua University, which is the MIT of China. I met with them in Beijing and their university press published the book in China. It would be very difficult to do this as a self-published author.

## Your Book Proposal

It's called a book proposal, a publishing proposal, submission, or a query letter. It tells the publisher what your book is about. Why should they publish your book? Why are you qualified to write it? How can you help to sell it?

Follow these steps to write a good book proposal:

- Understand the market. Go to Barnes & Nobles, Amazon, and other major bookstores and look at the existing books on your topic. What do they cover? What do they miss? When were they written? Has the market changed so there's opportunity for an updated book?

- Buy the books, read them, and take notes. Write a one-page summary of each book. Discuss strengths and weaknesses of each book and how you'll do it better or offer a different perspective. Include the book's title, author, publisher, year, and sales price. Publishers use to understand the opportunity. They also see how you write.

- Describe the size of your audience. Are there 10,000, 100,000, or 10,000,000 potential readers? Offer demographic data about the size of the audience.

- Describe your experience in writing. What have you written? Do you have project management experience? The publisher wants to know if you can meet deadlines.

- Show how you can help with marketing. Tell them how many contacts you have in your email list, LinkedIn contact list, Facebook, and so on. If you can participate in speaking events, say so. Will your company be willing to buy copies of the book?

Most publishers have submissions guidelines and forms on their website. You fill out the form and submit your proposal. They generally reply within a week.

I was lucky with my first few computer books because the market was growing and there were few writers. As I got experience, I learned what publishers wanted so I wrote better proposals for a book in the mid-90s. I researched the market and then sent a proposal to ten publishers. Every day, I waited by the mailbox for the replies. The first two arrived and these were rejections. No problem: eight hadn't yet replied. The next day, another rejection. A few days later, three more letters arrived. My wife, who was skeptical of the whole thing, watched me open them and said, "So three more rejections?" I said, "No, three accepted" and dropped them in her lap.

## What If You're Rejected?

Rejection doesn't have to do with you. Perhaps the publishers don't think there's a market for your topic. If you feel there is a market, look into self publishing at Amazon. You might also take their advice and look into writing something else.

How to Write a Book! by Andreas Ramos

## Delivering Your Manuscript to a Traditional Publisher

Many people think they have to finish the manuscript before they can look for a publisher. So they work for several years on the manuscript and then send it to a publisher.

However, most manuscripts are rejected. Either there are plenty of similar books, the publisher already has a book on the same topic, or the publisher doesn't think there's a market for it.

So don't write a manuscript. Write a proposal. If that's accepted, you can start writing. If it's rejected, you can try another topic.

## Changes to Your Proposal

There's another reason that you don't send finished manuscripts. Often, publishers know the market better than you and they'll want to make changes. If you deliver a completed manuscript, you're presenting a "take it or leave it" situation.

A proposal should be an opening for a conversation. How about we change this? Add that? The publishers have a sense of what bookstores are selling and they look for writers who can deliver that.

For example, you wrote a proposal for a book about opening a café in southern France with your cat. But the publisher knows ten books like that came out last year and nobody wants to hear about French café cats anymore. But… there's a hot new area: would you write about opening a coffee house in Sichuan with your dog? So you change everything and you have a book that sells.

## Multiple Submissions?

It used to be (long ago) you sent the manuscript to a publisher and waited for him to accept or reject before you contacted the next one. Some publishers rejected authors simply if they knew the author was talking to other publishers.

Things have changed. Today, it's normal for authors to submit their proposals to several publishers simultaneously. Some even hold auctions and let publishers bid against each other.

If it's a good proposal, you'll get a reply within a week or two.

## Royalties from a Publisher

In general, a publisher will give you 10% of the sales price for a paperback book, 15% for hardback, and 25% for ebooks. If the book sells more than (say) 2,000 copies, royalties may increase to 12%.

If you're famous (or notorious), you may get more than 10%. Stephen King can sell millions of books so he gets 25%, which is practically the entire profit of a printed book. That's one of the advantages of fiction: authors can sell hundreds of thousands of copies. In nonfiction, a best seller may sell only 5,000 books. That's minor sales compared to fiction authors.

Royalties are based on the selling price, not the cover price. Your book may go on the market for $45, but bookstores will sell it at a 30-50% discount. So if your $45 book sells for $22.50, you get 10% of $22.50, which is $2.25.

Once a quarter, the publisher adds up the sales, calculates your share, and a few weeks later, they send a check. If you got an advance, they deduct the royalties from the advance. If you publish with Amazon, you get an email statement at the end of the month and a deposit to your bank account.

## How Much Do You Make on Royalties?

In the movies, it looks like writers are millionaires. Ha! When I wrote my first book, I thought I'd make money on royalties. In reality, you get very little in royalties, whether you self publish or you write for a big publisher. You may get anywhere from a few thousand dollars to five or ten thousand dollars in a year. That may sound good, but when you add up the time, you earn more per hour at Burger Clown.

The secondary income can be more valuable. If your book is well-received, you may be offered speaking fees, consulting projects, and staff positions. All of this can advance your career. You may also be invited to join advisory boards. In return, you get pre-IPO stock.

None of this secondary income is automatic. How much you make in secondary income depends entirely on your efforts in promoting your career. If you deliver the book and wait under your bed, nothing will happen.

## Who Sets the Book's Price?

As part of your book proposal, you give your publisher a list of similar books. The publisher will check Nielsen Bookscan to see how the books are doing. They then set a price they think will be accepted by the target audience. You can make suggestions on the sales price, but the publisher will decide.

## Buying Books from Your Publisher

You can buy copies of your own book from your publisher. I bought my books which I sold at tradeshows or gave to friends, business prospects, and clients. You get an author's 50% discount of the sales price, so if the book sells for $25, you pay $12.50 (and shipping costs). I usually buy 100 books at a time.

## How Do Publishers Track Book Sales?

Publishers use *Nielsen Bookscan* to track book sales. Remember ISBN? Every book has an inventory tracking number. Nielsen Bookscan uses the ISBN to collect sales data from bookstore cash registers by book title, bookstore, city, and genre. Publishers can see at a glance where your book is selling. If it's doing well in California, they add more marketing there. If it's not selling in New York, they drop the marketing there. You can get access to Nielsen Bookscan in your Amazon Author Central account.

## What Does a Publisher Do?

So what does the publisher do? The writer writes and the publisher does everything else.

The publisher keeps an eye on the market, stays in touch with authors, reviews proposals, selects the books to be printed, manages the process, edits the drafts, and does the layout and cover. Publishers also handle production, printing, distribution, marketing, and accounting.

Publishing is geographically distributed. For one of my books, the project manager was in Florida, the copyeditors were in India, the graphics person was in San Francisco, and the layout person was in Los Angeles. The only one I ever met was the acquisitions editor. Everything else was by email.

Large publishers also have the resources to get the book to the major distributors such as Ingram and Bowker, which place the book in major bookstores across the country. The large publishers also have sales people who meet with college professors to get the book assigned as a textbook. They also carry out marketing campaigns to advertise the book.

However, some large publishers now leave the marketing entirely to the author. If you go with a publisher, you must make sure that you understand how they'll promote your book.

In general, a publisher handles many books. As the author, you only see your book and you assume it's a priority for them as well. But to them, your book is one of hundreds. An author said to me that a publisher is like a sea turtle that lays hundreds of eggs and then swims away. Only a few of the baby turtles make it to the water.

## What's the Biggest Problem with Publishers?

The weakest players in the world of books are the writers. They typically work alone and are paid only if their books sell. As you saw, few authors make meaningful money. Writers have little power.

If you look at writers' forums, you'll often see long rants from authors who hate their publisher. Some authors expect their publisher to host a book launch party on Times Square and place a stack of books in the window of every bookstore. Anything less and the authors think there's a conspiracy. Okay, some of these rants are pretty funny.

But publishers aren't there to make the author famous. If you work with a publisher (and I think it's totally fine to work with a publisher), then be clear about they do. Their job is to sell books. The publisher will produce the book (edit, layout, printing), do the marketing (press release, webpage, etc.), and arrange the distribution (placement into stores). They monitor the book's sales. If it sells, they do more promotion. If it doesn't sell, they move on to the next book.

You must collaborate with your publisher on promoting your book. See what they'll do, and add your own promotion so it doesn't contradict their work. Set up your own Google Adwords advertising, tweet about your book, create a webpage, and arrange your own speaking events. You should expect to spend at least 6-9 months on promotion after the publication date.

## Is Publishing a Good Business?

The publishing industry has turmoil in two areas: the technology and the business. People think Kindle and iPads are new, but we had Rocketbook in the late 90s. Publishing also went through a merger-and-acquisitions phase in the 80s and 90s. The rise of mega-bookstores (Borders, Barnes & Nobles, etc.) put the emphasis on blockbuster books. But Borders went bankrupt and thousands of bookstores closed. In the last few years, digital publishing changed everything again. Unknown authors sell hundreds of thousands of books on their own. Traditionally-published authors are walking away from their publishers and agents to start selling their own books.

It's hard to say what the future will be. The changes in technology, production, and distribution affect how writers, readers, agents, and publishers interact with each other.

The traditional publishers have a skill that nobody else has: they know how to bring good books to market. Perhaps publishers can evolve into seal of quality by acting as filters to select the best authors.

## Publishing Contracts

As the author, you start by owning all of the rights to your book. You assign part of those rights to others. For example, you assign the publishing rights to a publisher, the movie rights to a Bollywood studio, the theatrical rights to Broadway, and the game rights to Sony.

The publishing contract is an outline of what's expected from both the author and the publisher. You promise to deliver the finished manuscript by a certain date. You also promise that it's your original work and you have permission for the illustrations. If someone sues, you're liable.

In return, the publisher agrees to publish the work by a certain date. If they don't publish it or keep it in print, then the rights go back to you. The contract also states the amount of the advance, the royalties, and how this will be paid. Behind the legal talk, it's pretty straightforward. Any worthwhile publisher has published hundreds of books, so the contract will be standard.

## Publishing Contracts and Lawyers

Should you get a lawyer to review your contract? Since the contract is standard, there's very little that a lawyer can change.

Instead of talking with a lawyer, contact three or four of the publisher's authors and ask them if the publisher was fair and honest. If yes, just sign the contract. If no, find another publisher.

This brings up the so-called all-rights contract. Up until the 90s, book publisher only published books. But Star Wars was a new kind of thing. It included the movie, the books, the action figures, the board game, the computer game, the T-shirts, and other spin-offs.

Some publishers began to demand the rights to the book, the PDF, the ebook, the movie, the theatrical play, the cereal box toys, and the opera. This turned into the all-rights contract, as in, "we want all rights in every country in every format, including technologies not yet invented, in perpetuity."

The NWU, the Writers Guild, and other groups urge writers not to sign such contracts. As an author, you should assign only those rights to products that the publisher can actually deliver. If they want the rights to China, then see how much they've published in China. They want the movie rights? How many movies have they made? (This isn't far-fetched. I've written things that were later used in an opera in the UK).

## If I Self-Publish an ebook, Will a Publisher Notice Me?

Publishers want to sell books. If your self-published book is doing well, they'll approach you to publish it.

There are many examples of self-published books that have been picked up by traditional publishers. These include *Wool* by Hugh Howey, *50 Shades of Grey* by E. L. James, *Frontiers Saga* by Ryk Brown, and others.

## Summary of this Chapter

Until recently, the only path for a writer was to be chosen by a publisher. This was seen as validation: your book is good enough to be published.

This isn't trivial; I've often talked with people sneer at writers whose books weren't published by big publishers. Some writers struggled for years to get their books published. Some were rejected and spent a decade or more in deep depression.

This has changed. If a writer knows what she's doing, she can produce her books and reach her audience. Technology allows writers to print and sell books. There's something good in this for publishers. They can do what they do best: they understand the market; they can spot opportunities; they can bring forth the best writers; they can produce the best books for the market. Publishers can become a mark of quality.

## Interview with a Publisher: Roger Stewart

My name is Roger Stewart, and I'm currently an Editorial Director for McGraw-Hill Education (MHE). McGraw-Hill's headquarters are in New York City and I work in the San Francisco office. MHE can roughly be divided into the trade group (mhprofessional.com), which I belong to, and the school group (mheducation.com), which publishes textbooks and all sorts of other materials for educators. A trade publisher is one whose primary sales channel is bookstores. Of course, we publish books that crossover between the groups.

I've been in book publishing for 25 years, and I've acquired the rights to books on lots of different topics—including computing, electronic games, business, engineering, general nonfiction, and even a little bit of science fiction. These days I'm mostly acquiring books on computing topics and books for the TAB imprint, which are aimed at technical hobbyists and "makers." These include books on subjects such as DIY electronics, Arduino, 3D printing, and so on. Some of my more successful titles recently have included *Programming the Raspberry Pi*, *Practical Electronics for Inventors*, and *How to Diagnose and Fix Everything Electronic*.

I focus mostly on acquiring books for the print market. The eBook editions of the books we publish are significant factor now, but the overall ratio of sales is about 70% print and 30% digital.

How to Write a Book! by Andreas Ramos

## What about the Number of Pages?

Page count is an important consideration because the costs of copyediting, proofreading, layout, indexing, manufacturing, and even shipping are directly determined by the number of pages a book has.

Publishers typically create a profit-and-loss (P&L) spreadsheet to figure out how many copies of a book they have to sell at a particular price to achieve the proper price/earnings ratio. The price a publisher will charge is based on what the market will bear. If you're publishing in, say, trade paperback market where the going price for most books is $15 to $20, then your P&L pretty much has to work at that price point. If the P&L tells you the only way you can earn back your investment on an 800-page book in that market is $40 or $50 for it, then you may very well forego publishing that particular book because you run the risk of pricing yourself out of the market.

As an author, you should know your market. Look at other books that have been published in the same category. How are they priced? What's the typical page length? Are most of the books illustrated or text-only? Are they color or black-and-white?

If you're self-publishing ebook-only or ebook-and-POD, you probably want to keep the book short—under 200 pages—and the price low—under $10. Amazon is the biggest market for eBooks, so you would do well to study the Kindle best-seller lists to see what works.

## Do You Have a Source for Templates?

At McGraw-Hill, we ask authors to submit Word-compatible manuscripts, and we provide a few simple guidelines for writing to our house style or to series elements. Beyond that, if you can submit a clean, coherent document that addresses the right audience at the right level, we can handle the rest.

I edit mostly computing and technical books, and those kinds of books are usually illustrated with screen captures, photographs, drawings, and charts of various types. Many authors are tempted to submit their manuscripts as Word documents or PDFs with all of the illustrations inserted into the text. That's fine if you want to give the acquiring editor a sense of how the book will flow, but ultimately all of those illustrations will have to be submitted separately from the text. Some small-press publishers may be open to accepting layout files from the author, but larger publishers for the most part prefer to handle book design and layout themselves.

## Do You Work with Ghostwriters or Pseudonyms?

I rarely run into occasions where a ghostwriter or pseudonym is called for. But, from time to time, a writer will get in over his or her head and need help to complete the book. At such times, a co-author may be brought on—either credited or uncredited. Rarely are we willing change the overall terms of the deal in such cases, which means the original author will have to share the advance and royalties with the co-author.

## What's Your Experience with Book Agents?

Here's a little secret about publishing that you may not know. Editors want to publish your book. Finding good book proposals, signing agreements with authors, and publishing books is how we make our living. Without you, we don't have a job. So, anything that helps us find good authors and publish saleable books is welcome. A book agent who's willing be a partner in that quest is welcomed by a good acquiring editor.

## Describe an Ideal Book Proposal

If you poke around on their websites, you'll find that most publishers have guidelines describing what they're looking for in a proposal. Some may even provide you with a form to fill out. You should definitely tailor the proposal to the specific publisher whenever possible.

It's important that a proposal be well-written and clear in its intentions. If you can't write a readable proposal, what chance do you have of writing a readable book? On the other hand, of the proposal is well-written and interesting, the editor will be hooked regardless of whether or not you followed the guidelines.

## What Are the Advantages of Working with a Publisher?

I assume you're asking about the advantages of working with an established publisher versus self publishing. The answers to that question have perhaps become less clear now that eBook publishing platforms and print-on-demand services are more widely available to individuals. Of course, we've all heard stories of people like Hugh Howie who become huge successes in self publishing. But those stories are one-in-a-million.

According to an article published in Forbes last year, something like 600,000 to 1,000,000 books are published in the U.S. each year, and these days probably half of those are self-published. If you're lucky, you might expect to sell 200 to 300 copies of your self-published book. An established publisher can still give you distribution and credibility that most self-published authors can't achieve on their own. Besides that, you get professional marketing advice, copyediting, proofreading, cover design, and layout services that won't cost you a thing.

Even E.L. James, who was very successful as a self publisher, turned to established publisher Vintage for national bookstore distribution.

## How Many Books Should an Author Expect to Sell?

Would-be authors often ask me, "How many copies will my book sell?" At best, I can make a guess based on what similar books have sold—and my guess can be completely wrong. I've had the happy experience of publishing books that sold far more copies than I or anyone on the sales team anticipated, and I've had the unhappy experience of publishing a book that sold far fewer copies than we projected. Publishing is an art, not a science.

In my field of technical publishing, sales expectations can vary widely depending on the intended audience, subject matter, and level at which the text addresses the topic. For a general consumer-level audience, a publisher might expect to sell 5,000 to 10,000 copies and count the book a success. A very high-priced, very high-end technical book might sell only 1,000 or 2,000 copies and still be profitable.

## What's the Best Way to Publicize a Book?

Today in publishing the talk is all about author platforms. A "platform" is any way the author can reach an audience directly. The platform could be writing a column for a magazine, newspaper or website; producing a popular blog; conducting a lecture series; or making other public appearances.

Publishers tend to put the bulk of their resources toward producing and distributing books and promoting their brand or their product line rather than promoting individual mid-list authors and titles. In publishing as in everything else, however, success begets further success. If your book breaks out of the pack and sells better than expected, the publisher will likely "get behind it" with more promotional resources. The next edition of that book, or the next new book you write, will have greater resources thrown at it.

Until that happens, though, the best thing you can do is spend time pushing your book to every potential buyer or promotional venue you can think of. Pitch excerpts from your book or related articles to the kinds of magazines or websites that would be interested. Offer to give presentations at relevant events and to let yourself be interviewed by relevant media programs. Build a presence on social media websites. It's a lot of work, but if you make yourself known to relevant communities, people will look for your book.

In the end, you'll always be the best publicist for your own book. If you don't see that as part of the job of a writer, then you probably shouldn't pursue a career in writing books.

How to Write a Book! by Andreas Ramos

# 13. Selling Your Book: Preparation

## Introduction

It's good to be an author. It's even better if you're an author of best sellers. If you can ring that bell, you'll be able to sell many books and get lots of credibility and credentials. It will also increase sales of your past and future books. This chapter shows you on how to get your book to be an Amazon Best Seller.

## What's the Best Way to Publicize Your Book?

It's simple. Be an Amazon Best Seller or a New York Times Best Seller. That'll get lots of attention and you'll sell more books. That's the best publicity for your book.

**amazon** Best Seller

## How to Get Your Book to Be an Amazon Best Seller

So how do you get your book to be an Amazon Best Seller? Here's how:

- A month before the release day: Prepare for your book release. Set up a website, social media pages, and select the hashtags. Set up your monthly newsletter and clean your contact list. Identify your top influencers. Set up accounts for advertising at Google and Twitter. Prepare SEO for the search engines. Create ads for Google Adwords (both text and banner ads), Twitter, and LinkedIn. Set up web analytics.

- Set up the book for five days of free download at Amazon.

- On release day, turn on all promotion. Send out the newsletter. Turn on the ads in Google Adwords, LinkedIn, and Twitter. Be active in social media, including Facebook, Twitter, and LinkedIn. Use the links and hashtags in every posting. Send a new newsletter every other day.

- Watch Amazon every few hours. When your book shows up as a best seller, make a screenshot (be sure you know how to make and save screenshots!) Keep watching to see if your book moves higher.

- When it becomes a Best Seller, release new ads, tweets, Facebook postings, and send out yet another newsletter to get more people to download it. Watch to see if the ranking goes higher.

- Get reviews by offering a prize. For example, offer a $50 Amazon gift certificate, to be awarded by random drawing of the people who wrote a review.

Sales don't start slowly and then increase. Sales start with a bang and then decline sharply. So you must arrange all of your marketing to release simultaneously to get the maximum effect.

## Create a Calendar for Your Book Release

A book release will take about a month to prepare, a month to carry out, and up to six or nine months for follow up.

Use your calendar to plan this. The main steps are:

- Preparation. 30 days.

- Book release week. Five days.

- Follow up for speaking events, interviews, and other media engagement. Six to nine months.

## Your Digital Presence

Your goal in writing books is to build your reputation and credibility in your career. People should be able to find you, learn about you, and contact you. You do that by building *digital presence*, which means you manage how you appear on your website, your blog, email, newsletters, Facebook, LinkedIn, and Twitter. Make sure you're findable in all relevant sites.

Make sure that your message is consistent wherever you appear, including your website, Facebook page, and Twitter. You may have to go through each site and update your photo and information. Use the same photo of yourself in every site. You should also delete postings and photos that aren't relevant.

## Your Press Package

When you start doing speaking events or interviews, you'll need a press package. This is a collection of material that magazine editors and conference organizers can use to make a page about you for the article or conference. This includes the following:

- Photograph: Get a portrait photo by a professional photographer. Don't use a snapshot. Include large and small versions of your photograph that people can download.

- Statement: Like the elevator pitch, this is a short 3-5 word summary. This is what your friends will tell others about you.

- Short bio: This may be four bullet points about you

- A list of events and conferences where you've spoken

- A list of your books and magazine articles

- Contact information: Make it easy for people to contact you. Put your email address and telephone number on your website. Include the city so people know your time zone.

## Your Book in a One Sentence

When people look at your book, you think they're wondering, "What's your book about?"

But that's the wrong question. What they're really asking is, "What's in it for me?", "How is this going to benefit me?", and "How will it solve my problems?"

A way to do this is to write a short 4-5 line summary about your book. When you've finished, cut the number of words by half. When you've done that, do it again. This forces to you say the key point in a few words. Your book should be about one clear idea, not two or three.

Another way to develop your key idea is to stand at a trade show and say it to people who stop at your booth. You'll say it perhaps 100 times in a day. You'll see in people's eyes if they're interested or not. You'll learn to get straight to the point and say it in a few words.

## Your Website

You need a website. The easy solution is WordPress. The point is to let your visitors be able to read about you, your book, and where to get the book. You should also add your press package and contact information so clients, agents, and publishers can reach you.

Should you have one site for all of your books or build a separate site for each book? I built a website for each of my first seven books. But seven sites meant my web traffic was split among those sites. The better solution is one site (such as yourname.com) for all books. When someone comes to your site, she'll see that you have additional books. Visit my site to see how I did this.

## The Webpage for Your Book

At your website, add a page for your book. It should have a short summary of your book, several bullet points with the key benefits, and the book's cover.

- Give away a chapter: Offer the best chapter as a PDF. This shows your reader what you can do and she'll come back for the rest. At the back of the chapter, include your contact information.

- Give away the whole book: You can also offer the entire book as a PDF. At the back of the book, place your contact information.

- Make the book's URL easy to remember and type, such as "yourname.com/lawbook."

- You can also offer templates, documents, reports, worksheets, a list of resources, questions to ask, and interviews. These can be as free or paid files. Let people know these are available and you'll get lots of visitors.

As soon as you start working on your book, you should set up the webpage. Let people know the book is coming so they can sign up for the newsletter.

## Add Your eBook to Amazon Kindle Direct Publishing

Here's a short summary for the process to place your ebook at Amazon. Amazon Kindle Direct Publishing (KDP). Use KDP for selling your ebook at Amazon. Your ebook can be read on Kindle, iPads, all tablets, all smart phones, and in web browsers on laptops and computers.

- Have the book file ready to upload. It can be a Word file.

- You also need a cover illustration. You can either have a cover to upload, or you can use KDP's cover creation tool. If you have a cover, it should be in JPG or TIFF format.

- If you use an ISBN number, have that ready too. You use one ISBN for the print book, another for the ebook, and another for the PDF (in other words, a different ISBN for each version of your book).

- Sign up at kdp.amazon.com

- Fill out the form. It's straight-forward: enter the title, subtitle, ISBN, and so on.

- Add the name of contributors. Enter your name as the author, plus tnames and roles of others, such as illustrators, editors, and so on.

- Choose up to two categories. For the #TwitterBook, I chose BUSINESS & ECONOMICS > E-Commerce > Internet Marketing and COMPUTERS > Web > Social Networking.

- Add up to seven keywords. Use SEO tools to find keywords that have lots of searches.

- Upload your book cover in JPG or TIFF format.

- KDP asks if you want to enable digital rights management (DRM). I recommend you select "do not enable." DRM just causes problems for people.

- Upload your book file. I send it as a Word document. Amazon will convert it into a Kindle file. This may take up to twelve hours. Amazon KPD will send you an email when it's ready.

- When the file is ready, Amazon KPD will show you possible misspelled words and ask you to confirm them.

- Choose the countries in which you want the book to be offered. You can choose worldwide or by country.

- Enter your list price. This can be between $0.99 and $200.

- Choose your royalty. Do you want a small royalty or a BIG royalty? In some countries, Amazon is obligated to pay a higher royalty, so a table will show you the royalty amount and your share, along with the sales price and royalty after exchange rate conversion, along with applicable sales or

VAT tax. Read the section in this book on pricing ("How Do I Set the Price?").

- Finally, you confirm that you have the rights to the book.

When you click submit, it can take two to twelve hours for your book to appear in Amazon. You'll get a notification by email. When that shows up, go back to your KDP account and check for any messages.

At step #6 in KDP, you can preview your book. Scroll through the book and look for problems in the layout. I set it to an iPad display with small font and scroll through the text.

You can make changes to your book and upload a new file. It may take a few hours for the new version to be available. After you've uploaded the new version, check the layout again.

When you make changes, upload them late at night while people are sleeping. If you upload during the day, your page won't be available and you'll lose sales.

## Amazon KDP Select

When you post your digital book at Amazon KDP, you can add *Amazon KDP Select*. For 90 days, your book gets more promotion at Amazon. It will be offered to Amazon Prime members, who can read it for free (you get a fee).

The most important feature of KDP Select is the *Free Book Promotion* option, which allows you to give your book out for free for five days at Amazon. You use this to get lots of downloads. Although the downloads are free, they count as sales. This is how you get your book to be an Amazon Best Seller.

When you enroll in KDP Select for your book, it's effective for 90 days. You can cancel at any time. At the end of 90 days, it rolls over for another 90 days. You can turn this on and just leave it on.

To set up a five-days-free offer:

- Enroll in KDP Select. If you just added your book, you'll have to wait a few hours before you can select this.

- When KDP is active, click on Manage Benefits.

- Choose a *Free Book Promotion* or a *Kindle Countdown Deal*. The free book promotion lets you pick up to five days in a 90-day period. You can select two days here and three days there, or just pick all five days in one week. As for the countdown deal, that's a time-based promotional discount. Customers see the discount and the time remaining at that price point (for example, $2.99 for two days only).

- Choose the days for the promotion. I suggest you pick Monday to Friday. Don't select a week near a major holiday.

You can choose a five-day period several weeks away and then prepare all of the marketing and newsletters to coincide with the promotion.

Upload your book on a Wednesday but don't announce it. This gives you time to make any changes. Announce the book release for Monday (which means after midnight, between Sunday and Monday).

## Adding Your Print Book to Amazon CreateSpace

Use Amazon CreateSpace to sell your print book as a paperback or hardback.

Here's a summary of CreateSpace Amazon:

- Prepare the book's back cover. There's a standard layout for these, so look at similar books in your field by major publishers. (To see an example, download this book's cover from the book's webpage.)

- Determine the width of the spine for the side of your book. Put the book title, your name, and your publishing logo on the spine. If you're using white paper, multiply the number of pages by 0.002252. For example, 179 pages X 0.002252 = 0.403108."

Just as with the digital version, go ahead and upload a test book to Amazon CreateSpace. Go through the steps to learn how to do this.

If Amazon's computer won't accept your file, contact their support. They can fix problems for $99.

## *Your Email Newsletter*

The best way to reach your audience with through email. Yes, email. Why? A McKinsey study shows email is nearly forty times more effective for acquiring customers than social media (for more, see http://goo.gl/BU28Fv).

The other benefit of an email newsletter is control of the data. You can build a list of 100,000 people in Facebook, but Facebook, not you, owns your list. When you post to Facebook, your message will be shown to only 9% of your list. How can you reach the other 91%? You have to pay Facebook. Which of the 9% saw your message? Facebook won't tell you who saw it or not.

By using an email service provider (ESP) such as MailChimp or ConstantContact, you own your list. When you send an email newsletter, every subscriber gets a copy. You get a report on how many people opened the email and how many clicked on the links. You can also see which people opened (or didn't open) the newsletter. You can delete inactive subscribers. People can also unsubscribe on their own.

## How to Create Your Newsletter List

You'll need to build your list of subscribers. Here is how to do this:

- Export your contacts from Gmail and save as an Excel file. In Gmail: Go to Contacts | More | Export. Save as Outlook CSV.

- Export your contacts from LinkedIn. Save them as an Excel file. To do this in LinkedIn: Go to Network | Contacts | Gear icon | Export LinkedIn Connections. Save as Outlook CSV.

- Use a business card scanner to add business cards to a spreadsheet file. There are also apps for smart phones which let you take photos of cards and convert them into text.

- Combine your lists into a master list. Delete duplicates. You only need first name, last name, and email address.

- You then *scrub the list*. That means you use a tool to test each address to see if it's active. As many as 30% of people move or abandon email addresses each year. If you don't scrub the list, you'll send out the newsletter, get hundreds of bounced emails, your email service provider will think you're a spammer, and your email account will be shut down. To scrub the list, you upload your list to a list scrubber and after a few hours, it sends a report on which emails are active or inactive. You can use a list scrubber at DataValidation.com for about $7 for 1,000 email addresses. Delete the bad email addresses. You can send your email newsletter to emails that are marked both good and maybe.

- You may want to review the final list to make sure you want to reach these people. Some email addresses may be family, your bank, and so on.

- To send a newsletter to the list, you can use email tools such as Constant Contact or MailChimp. I suggest MailChimp because the first 2,000 names are free. It also has tools for managing your list.

Don't send from your email account at Gmail or Yahoo. Most email services won't let you send more than 400 emails per day. They also don't like spammers. If you go over 400, they may shut down your account. Email also lacks tools to manage your list.

It's pretty easy to set up an email newsletter template at MailChimp. Once you've set up the template, you can send out a monthly email in ten minutes.

Here are a few tips for your newsletter:

- Send newsletters in the middle of the day, in the middle of the week and in the middle of the month. That's when people are at work, which means they're not doing anything.

- Don't send near holidays. Don't send during a short workweek. People are thinking about their days off and they won't read your newsletter. Or they read it, go on vacation, and forget about you.

- Open your calendar and select the delivery dates for the next twelve months.

- Offer free stuff to get more subscribers. Give away books, PDFs, chapters, templates, reports, and worksheets.

You must download your LinkedIn contact list right now. At the moment, you can download it, but LinkedIn can block this whenever they like. You'll lose that list. Stop reading and download it now.

For example, I have 1,921 contacts in LinkedIn. I downloaded the contact list, scrubbed the emails, and found that 5% (96 email accounts) were dead email addresses. I then sent out a email newsletter to 1,825 people. Of those, 32% (584 people) opened the newsletter. I sent this every month for three months and then deleted the email addresses which never opened the newsletter. I ended up with 524 LinkedIn contacts who want to hear from me.

## How to Write a Good Newsletter

You may be wondering, aren't email newsletters boring? Don't people ignore those? Several years ago, I was a director at Acxiom. It's one of the largest email marketing company in the world. It sends out billions of emails every month for Fortune 500 clients. Here are a few basic pointers:

- Keep it short. Two or three lines is good. People ignore long emails.

- Focus on your reader. Give him something that's a benefit for him. Don't talk about you. Nobody cares about you. Okay, your dog cares about you. I have a cat. Believe me, cats don't care.

- Be personal. Nobody reads boring corporate stuff. Write as if you're writing to friends.

- Send something every month. People get used to your emails and they'll look forward to the next one.

## SEO for Your Book

You use SEO (search engine optimization) to make sure people can find your book in search engines such as Google, Yandex, Baidu, and Bing.

The best way to do SEO is to find out what your audience wants and write a good book for them. Send your book to people who know you. If they find it useful, they'll tell their friends. Their friends will tell more friends. They'll post it to their blogs and websites. The search engines will index those pages and more people will see it.

You can get a free copy of my SEO eBook at andreas.com.

## Set Up Digital Advertising

Digital advertising is the best way to quickly reach a large audience. Create a few ads and place them in Google, LinkedIn, Twitter, Bing, Facebook, StumbleUpon, Instagram, and other sites.

You set up advertising accounts in each one. You can get $50 or $100 in free credit when you start an account in most of these sites. Search for (for example) "$50 free credit in Twitter."

Set the launch dates in the accounts. You can also pick the locations where your ads will appear. If your budget is small, select the five largest states in the USA (California, Texas, Florida, New York, and Illinois). If people in these states like your book, they'll talk about it and that'll reach the remaining states.

To use digital advertising effectively, look at key performance indicators (KPI) such as cost-per-lead (CPL) and cost-per-acquisition (CPA). Get my *KPI eBook* at Andreas.com.

## Set Up Social Media

Social media allows people to find others in their community and talk together. This means social is a great way to participate in an interest community. Social sites include Facebook, LinkedIn, WeChat, Twitter, Tumblr, StumbleUpon, and Instagram.

To decide where to put your efforts, look at your web analytics and see which social sites are sending traffic to you. You can't assume which social site will work best. I use Facebook and Twitter, yet StumbleUpon sends me twice as much traffic as all other social sites combined.

For more about Twitter, read *#TwitterBook*. Free copy at Andreas.com.

## Pick Your Hashtags

You should also develop a hashtag for your book. Hashtags, such as #authors, are used on Twitter and other social sites so people can build conversation communities. You can learn more about hashtags in my *#TwitterBook*.

It's easy to find hashtags. You can enter a hashtag at Hashtagify.me to find additional hashtags.

For example, I used Hashtagify.me to looked for hashtags for this book. I also used Topsy.com to find how many people have used that hashtag in the last thirty days. I found #selfpublish (1,600 uses in the last 30 days), #selfpubl (11,000), #pubtip (10,000), #writers (65,000), #indiepub (11,000), #author (170,000), #amwriting (65,000), and #writing (179,000).

You'll notice the most obvious hashtag (#selfpublish) was used only 1,600 times in thirty days. The hashtag #amwriting (as in, "I am writing") was used 65,000 times. This lets you find the best hashtag to reach your audience.

## What about Content Marketing?

Traditional marketing is called push marketing where the information is pushed at the audience, whether they want it or not. A study by Acxiom found 80% of digital advertising is ignored by people. They don't notice text ads or banner ads. Digital advertising is becoming increasingly expensive and ineffective.

Content marketing, in contrast, is based on offering high-quality information which the audience, on its own, seeks and shares among themselves. Content marketing answers the audience's own questions from their point of view.

Content marketing has several advantages:

- Cheaper distribution because the audience will distribute it for you. The cost of distribution for content marketing is less than 10% of traditional marketing. Just create it, distribute a few digital copies to high-visibility influencers, and watch it be distributed for free.

- Lower cost of advertising because it bypasses advertising in search engines, newspapers, etc.

- It works better with SEO because search engines give preference to non-commercial or unbiased information

To learn more, get my book *The Big Book of Content Marketing.*

## How to Find Your Influencers

As I pointed out earlier, 1% of the people in a field are followed by everyone else. If you reach the 1%, the rest will see it. These people are called influencers.

Find the influencers, contact them, and let them know what you're doing. If the influencers think it's valuable, they'll share it to their audiences.

Have the list of influencers ready for release day. Write a short email that contains the book title, the shortened URL, and the hashtag. Write the email so the influencers only have to copy it and pass it along to their readers.

There are a number of tools to find influencers, such as BuzzSumo, AuthoritySpy, and Traackr. New tools appear (and disappear) every few months.

Be careful with influencer tools. Activity on Facebook, Twitter, and other social sites is easy to fake. Some people are ranked highly even though they're not really influential. I suggest you use several tools to create and compare lists.

The tools help you to get started by creating lists. You'll have to evaluate each person to create a useful list.

### Get Blurbs

A book blurb is a short sentence fragment by a leading expert that goes on the cover of your book. People pay attention to blurbs from well-known persons. Try to get several blurbs by leading people in your field. Contact them, send them ARCs, and ask them for blurbs.

### FTC Rules about Compensation to Influencers

Be careful with payments for blurbs or endorsements. The US Federal Trade Commission (FTC) requires influencers to state if they received payment, products, gifts, trips, or similar. Penalties can be US$250,000 or more per incident.

See *FTC Guidelines on Testimonials and Endorsements* or go to http://1.usa.gov/13U7Uin for more. There's similar legislation in other countries.

By the way, Google doesn't like this either. If they notice you're paying to have people talk about you on the web, they may blacklist you.

### Promote Your Book before You Publish

Let people know that you're working on a book. Talk about this in your newsletter, blog, tweets, and so on. Let people know they can subscribe to your newsletter to be notified when it's ready. You can start promoting the book long before you publish. Some authors start a year ahead.

### Be Ready Before Publication

You must have all of this ready before you release the book. The goal is to get an Amazon Best Seller, which you do by bringing lots of people at the same time to your book at Amazon. You can do that only if you have everything ready to go.

It can take a busy two or three weeks to set up all of this. If you've never done it, it can take two or three months. Of course, you're doing this at the same time that you're editing and finishing your book.

Most people write the book, release it, and then start working on the marketing. Well, that's like starting a party and then sending out the invitations. If it takes a month to set up marketing, the book will be old news by the time you announce it. So you have to prepare your marketing before the book is ready.

## Summary of this Chapter

As you can see, it's quite a bit of work to sell your book. You have to learn and use a number of marketing tools. That's why many writers choose to let the publisher do the marketing. However, for nonfiction writers, the point is to build your career, so I think you should manage as much of your marketing as you can. If you do only one thing, then send out your monthly newsletter.

Does this really work? If you do a good job with your webpage, newsletter, and social media (Facebook, Twitter, LinkedIn), you won't need to advertise. This book became an Amazon Best Seller at #2 in two categories on its first day without any paid advertising, not even a penny.

# The Author Speaks: Susan Levitt

Susan Levitt is the author of five books published in eight languages including the best sellers *Taoist Astrology* (Destiny Books, 1997) and *The Complete Tarot Kit* (U.S. Games Systems Inc., 2012). Susan is a professional astrologer, tarot reader, and feng shui consultant in the San Francisco Bay Area. She's been featured on CNN, was voted Best Astrologer by *SF Weekly* in San Francisco, and was interviewed on the television program *Chicagoing*. She holds a B.F.A. from The School of the Art Institute of Chicago.

## Why Do You Write?

I write because I have ideas and I have a lot to say! I have a strong point of view. I write about what interests me. Writing has always been my path. I could read when I was three. My older sister learned to read at five, I watched over her shoulder and picked it up immediately. My childhood existed in Victorian England and feudal Russia. I loved Lewis Carrol, Dickens, and Tolstoy. I became very interested in languages, applied myself at school, and skipped three grades. I supported myself as an English tutor and writer of college papers during two undergrad degrees and grad school. I kept learning how to write better by reading great authors.

## How Has Writing Affected Your Life and Career?

I started studying astrology when I was eleven. When I was 17, I had my first tarot card reading. I developed an interest in metaphysics and started writing about it. Writing has affected my career by giving me professional credibility. "She wrote 5 books!" seems to put people at ease about my credentials.

## Do You Prefer Self Publishing or Traditional?

Traditional. Let them do the distribution! But self publishing can work too, especially for books on a specialized topic. Just be aware about self-publishing operations are actually vanity presses. Yes, you have a book, but they'll publish anything if you pay them.

## How Did You Find and Choose Your Publisher?

I wrote reviews of spiritual books that I liked. A publisher of spiritual books, Inner Traditions, sent me their catalog because I was on their radar from reviewing a couple of their titles. I liked their list so I sent them some notes that I had about Chinese astrology. I'd been working on the notes thinking the material could be used in Chinese medicine schools in the west. And I had some Chinese astrology notes that I gave to clients who came to me for astrology readings. I sent my notes to Inner Traditions on Monday, and in the mail on Friday was a book contract. I added more text and they they published my first book *Taoist Astrology*, which was the first Four Pillars book in English. *Taoist Astrology* was so successful they asked me to write *Taoist Feng Shui* and *Teen Feng Shui*. Inner Traditions attends the yearly Foreign Rights book fest in Hamburg, Germany. They sold the foreign rights to all three of my books that are now published in eight languages.

Something similar happened when I was published by U.S. Games Systems, Inc. I was teaching tarot classes and made copies of info to hand out to students. I was hassled at a Kinko's about intellectual copyright when copying tarot cards. So I sent my class notes to the publishing house that owns almost all tarot imagery and tarot decks. I just wanted to find out how I could copy the cards, but they sent me a book contract. Together we designed *The Complete Tarot Kit*. It was an international best seller. My tarot book *Introduction To Tarot* that was part of the kit was published separately a year later.

## Did You Start with Traditional or Self-Publishing?

I'm grateful my five books were with reputable publishers who are respected in their fields. But today I self publish my writings in social media and blogs.

### What's Your Experience with Self Publishing?

So far with self publishing, it's all been good. For material that I publish online, I'm glad it's still free to post. I like the convenience of going to my web site and changing text at any time. I also appreciate that I receive monthly payments from internet astrology sites where I provide articles, such as Astrology.com and ChineseAstrologyOnline.com. I email my text and they post it.

### What's Your Experience with Traditional Publishing?

I really didn't have bad experiences with traditional publishers. But I they were slow, and not early adopters of new technology. Some publishers still take orders by fax.

### Do You Have an Agent?

I don't need an agent, and the handful of agents that I've met didn't seem insightful or well read. If publishers want to publish my books, they deal with me directly.

### Did a Lawyer Review Your Contract?

I read my contract thoroughly and didn't require legal counsel. I felt relieved that as a writer I didn't end up writing anything I didn't want to write.

### What's the Best Way to Promote Your Book?

The publishing houses did that for me. But a very old-fashioned marketing tool, word of mouth, really worked for me. My books have a cult following.

### What Would You Have Done Differently?

Nothing.

# 14. Selling Your Book: Book Release

Okay, the big day is here. You have the book ready to go. You can stop relaxing. Spit in your hands and let's get to work. It's going to be a busy week.

## The Release Day

Let's say you release the book on June 1st. What's that actually mean?

The book comes out when Amazon's computers release it. Amazon is in Seattle (which is on the Pacific west coast), so it uses Pacific Standard Time (PST). Your book will be available one minute after midnight, between May 30th and June 1st. That's 3 am in NYC, 9 am in Paris, noon in Iran, 1:30 pm in India, and 4 pm in China. This matters because when you release the book for free download, most of the day is already over in Asia.

This means you have to consider the calendar carefully. You should release early in the week to get five business days. Never release on a Thursday or Friday. Don't release before or after a major holiday.

## Contact Influencers

Send an email to your influencers. These are people who have lots of followers via newsletters, blog, or Twitter. Let them know they can give the book for free to their followers. Tell them the price will go up after five days.

## Send the Email Newsletter

On release day, stay up until midnight Seattle time. Send the newsletter after midnight. People around the world will get your email. In the email, write the book is free at Amazon for one week only. Include a link to the book.

## Post to Your Blog, Facebook, Twitter, LinkedIn...

Tell your followers the book is free at Amazon. You can post sections of your book at your blog. For the five free days at Amazon, pick five useful sections of your book. It's easy if you're using Wordpress. Just copy from Word and paste into Wordpress. It automatically converts the text into the right format. At the top and bottom of the blog posting, add links to the book at Amazon. Set the publishing schedule for the day of the week it should appear.

You can use third-party interfaces to manage Twitter. This allows you to set up tweets which are sent later. Hootsuite lets you write a series of tweets which will be sent on book release day and the next four days. You can also use hashtags to let discussion groups know about your book.

## Turn On the Ads

This one is easy because you can set up the advertising ahead of time to turn itself on and off.

The ads turn on at midnight at the beginning of the day and turn off at the end of the day at midnight. For example, they turn on at 00:01 am of June 1st and turn off at 11:59 pm on June 5th (that's 23:59 pm).

Luckily, the three computers that matter are all on the US West Coast (Pacific Standard Time) so you only have to deal with one time zone. Amazon's computer is in Seattle, Twitter in San Francisco, and Google and LinkedIn are in Silicon Valley.

## Watch Your Rank at Amazon

During those five days, you need to watch your ranking at Amazon like a cat watches a mouse hole. You want to see how high your book reaches. If it hits #10, don't quit. Keep watching. It may go to #6. Refresh Amazon every hour.

Each time it goes higher, make a screen shot and save it. Once it peaks, it drops quickly. You'll be able to use that screen shot in your subsequent marketing.

## What Does It Take to Be a #1 Best Seller?

Remarkably, it doesn't take many books to be a best seller. At any moment, there may be a few dozen books in your category. Most of those are several years old, so they may only sell a few copies each month. If you sell a few hundred books in five days, you'll be the best seller for that category.

At Amazon, free copies also count in your sales. This means you only have to get 500-1,000 free downloads within a short time period.

This also means it's important that you choose your category carefully. If you select a broad topic, there may be lots of competition. The narrower your category, the easier it's to get a high ranking.

## Change Your Price after Six Days

To create a sense of value, set a high sales price, such as $20 or $25. This lets you create an offer that has both value ("Get a $25 book for free") and a sense of urgency (Get it free now! Five days only!) After a few weeks, drop the price of the ebook to $2.99.

### But How Do You Make Money If It's Free?

The best price for your readers of course is free. By offering your book for free, people will flock to Amazon to download it. Because it's a free-this-week-only offer, people will tell others in Twitter, email, and so on. Those free downloads count towards your sales, so you'll rank high in Amazon.

Remember, you don't make money on books. Books create opportunities such as speaking fees, consulting fees, projects, jobs, and pre-IPO stock for advisory boards. You get asked to join a team to start a company. All of this is worth more than book sales.

### Summary of this Chapter

After months of preparation, your release week will go by in a flash. Have everything ready, turn it on, and watch.

# 15. Selling Your Book: Follow Up

After the release, you continue to promote your book. You should expect to spend six to nine months in marketing after the book is released. You'll send out books, speak at events, and do interviews.

A few months after the book release, start planning your next book.

## Order 100 Books

You should buy perhaps one hundred books. You'll send books to conferences to arrange speaker events and interviews on radio shows and in newspapers and magazines. You'll also send books to influencers, your team, friends, and business friends.

If you're suddenly invited to speak at an event, you should have at least fifty books ready to go. Shipping can take several weeks, so have enough on hand.

## Send Books to Your Team

You should send an autographed book to each person on the team. You should also acknowledge them in your book.

## Give Books to Friends, Family, and Colleagues

Your friends, family, and colleagues will recommend you to others. So give them signed copies of your book.

Authors share books with each other. If they give you a copy of their book, give them one of your books.

### How to Send Books by Mail

When you send books by mail, be sure to send them in a way they won't be damaged. If you put it in a bubble envelop or wrap it in brown paper, the edges will be damaged or bent when the book falls and hits a corner.

To test this, I sent books in various envelopes to myself. The best solution was to put the book between two sheets of cardboard that overlap the book by two inches. That protects the corners. Use shipping tape to seal all four sides and use a large paper envelope.

You can send books via book rate (called *media mail* in the USA). This means you pay low postage. Talk with the post office about the criteria for this. The delivery time for media mail depends on holidays. If you send in mid-November or later, your book may be delayed until January. It'll also undergo rough handling because of large packages.

### Use Social Media for Your Book

You can use social media tools, such as Facebook, LinkedIn, and Twitter to stay in touch with your audience. Let people know in your book where they can find you online. You can post updates, talk about book events, answer questions, and discuss new topics.

### Update Your Digital Book

One of the cool things about digital books is that you can update the book. After you release the book, people may find errors or items to change. No problem. Upload a new version of your book to replace the old version. Notify the team at Kindle Direct Publishing. Tell them what you changed. If it's substantial, they'll notify customers.

This is why I use version numbers and release dates for the book. I also put a notice in the book for people to check for new versions every six months or yearly.

## Offer Your Book on Your Website

You can also distribute the book on your site:

- Offer a book in return for registration at your website: When they register with their name and email, they get a copy of the book.

- Sell books with PayPal: PayPal accepts all credit cards. Best of all, you get 100% of the sale (minus a small transaction fee).

- Sell books on your website with Amazon: At Amazon, you can get a button that you put on your site. Customers click the button and it brings them to Amazon, where they can pay for your book.

- Sell your book at other websites: You can get affiliate buttons at Amazon which you can give to other websites. When someone clicks at that website to buy your book, the website gets a percentage of the sale.

Amazon handles ordering, payment, delivery, and returns. They also take care of problems with credit card payments, damaged books, and lost mail.

You can also sell books with Smashwords, Lulu, and many other book sites. I use Amazon to keep it simple. Visit these sites to learn more.

## Speaking Events and Speaking Fees

The best presentation is where you tell your audience the most useful information. Answer the person's hidden question, "What's in it for me?" They'll come to your site for more. Your audience will tell others about you.

When you speak at an event, don't sell. People aren't interested in advertisement for your products or services. Don't hold back or say, "You'll have to buy the book to find out."

I always give the audience free digital copies of my book. I give them a link where they can download it or I give a copy to the event organizers to send to attendees. Your audience will distribute your book for you.

You should bring a few boxes of books so people can buy books. The speaking fees depends on the size of the group and the type of organization. Generally, local events may give you a bottle of wine or a box of chocolate as a thank-you. To get in the professional speaking circuit, join the National Speakers Association (NSASpeaker.org). These engagements generally pay $3,000 to $5,000 or more, plus expenses.

To speak at events:

- Make a list of relevant local organizations, business groups, business associations, and colleges.

- Reach out to organizations. They're always looking for speakers. If you know someone at the association, ask them to recommend you to the directors.

- Contact them ahead of your book release. Their speaker's calendar generally is filled three to six months in advance.

- Send a book, a summary of the book, your bio, your photo, and a list of where you've spoken

## Bookstore Speaking Events

If your book was printed by a traditional publisher, you can also speak at local bookstores. Contact the bookstores and ask for the person who schedules the speaking events. Send your press package and a copy of your book. These events are generally booked three to four months in advance. So if you want to speak in the same month that your book comes out, you need to plan ahead.

Give a short presentation on the key ideas in your book that are useful for your audience, and then open it up for questions and discussion.

After you finish your talk, you can sign your books. Bring at least two pens to sign books. Pens tend to disappear.

The bookstore will also sell your book, so have several boxes of books for them.

To promote the event, send out newsletters, use local advertising in Google and Twitter, and put up flyers in cafés.

## Your Book at Tradeshows and Conferences

Other venues are tradeshows and conferences. If you know a company will have a booth at a tradeshow or conference, talk with the vice president of marketing to see if you can be at their booth. They need a draw to attract people, so you can be there with a large poster and a stack of your books. Talk with attendees and give them a signed book in exchange for their business card.

The company will pay for your books, travel expenses, and trade show entrance fees. You'll also get a copy of the business cards for your mailing list. You should also run Google and Twitter ad campaigns to announce that you'll be giving away books at the conference.

## Posters of Your Book

For events, make large posters of your book cover. Send a PDF of the cover to a copy store and they'll print it on paper or foam board. I recommend foam board; it looks better and lasts longer. The larger, the better. I use three-feet tall (1 meter) posters.

## Interviews with Radio, TV, Magazines, Newspapers

When you're interviewed by radio, TV, magazines, and newspapers, you'll find you have very little time to say much. Thirty minutes goes by very fast with station breaks and announcements. Pick one good idea and explain it. That's about all the time you'll have.

Interviewers may ask for a copy of your book in advance, but they'll rarely have time to read it. So help them out by sending them a list of ten or fifteen questions and answers. Remember your research in the social question-and-answer sites? That's a source for good questions. Write these in a natural talking voice, not written questions.

If you work with a traditional publisher, they may arrange interviews. You should also reach out to media yourself. Find radio and TV shows relevant to your topic and contact the programming manager. Send a short email (two or three lines) with a link to your book and press package. Tell them why their audience will be interested in your book.

Be ready. The media works on short notice. You may be asked to go on in 45 minutes. You won't have time to prepare. I've spoken on the BBC and NPR with 15 minutes notice. At conferences, I'm often asked to do TV interviews. "May we interview you? Great! Just turn around and face the camera. Ready? Go. What led you to write this?"

So, really, before your book is published, write your talking points and know them by memory.

Newspapers and magazines in Central Europe, China, and South America will email you a list of questions. You can also add questions or improve the questions. Generally, your interview will be translated, so use simple English and avoid unnecessary technical terms or jargon which may be difficult to translate.

You can post copies of your presentations or interviews to your blog.

## How to Get an Article in a Magazine

You can also write articles for magazines or major blogs. Just as with speaking events, look for magazines and blogs with substantial reach. Use influencer tools to find these. Write to the editor and state your credential, experience, and reach. Send your press package and a copy of the book. Offer a few topics and be open to suggestions.

## Interviews with Graduate Students

You may also be contacted by graduate students for their thesis. They'll send you a list of questions. You can edit their questions or add new questions. In contrast to media interviews, a thesis interview requires substantial informational replies, so write several paragraphs to each question. Include sources and additional material.

## Speaking Tours around the World

As you build your reputation and credibility, conferences in other countries will invite you to speak. Generally they offer a speaking fee and cover travel expenses. I've spoken at events in Paris, Vienna, Copenhagen, Brussels, Beijing, Shanghai, Berlin, NYC, Saudi Arabia, and Mexico City.

## My Blog Is Getting Traffic. How Can I Make Money?

When you have books, a blog, and a website, you'll start to get lots of visitors to your website. People ask me if they can make money with their blog traffic.

To do this, you use Google Adsense to place advertising in your website or blog. You sign up and download a few lines of code, which you place in your website or blog. When people look at your webpage, Google shows the ads. The ads are related to your page, so if you wrote about Hawaii, there'll be ads for flights and hotels.

How much can you make with advertising on your website? I've been using Adsense on Andreas.com since 2003. Here are numbers from my website.

As the advertiser (you're using advertising to sell your products), you buy ads by the CPM price. CPM is Cost per Mille (where "mille" is one thousand in Latin). If the CPM is $8, you pay $8 to have your ad shown to a thousand people. If you want ten thousand people to see your ad and the CPM is $8, then you pay $80.

The same thing works in reverse for the publisher (the publisher is the site that shows the advertising. For example, a publisher is a web magazine that shows an ad for Honda). The publisher wants to know how much he gets for the ad, so instead of CPM, he uses RPM (Revenue per Mille), which means how much he gets for every thousand viewers.

On average, I get $100 from Google for 15,000 visitors, which means Google Adsense pays me US$0.0067 per unique visitor (the amount varies, depending on the ads, the site, and so on). I get $6.67 RPM.

If the CPM is $8 and the RPM is $6.67, then Google Adsense gets the difference ($1.33). That's how Google Adsense makes money. Google Adsense is an ad distribution network (ADN). There are dozens of ADNs. Google Adsense has the largest share of the US market. When you look for an ADN to place their ads on your site, ask for the RPM so you can compare the offer.

Are you beginning to see the problem? To get meaningful revenue, say, $2,000 per month, you need 300,000 unique monthly visitors. That's a huge amount of traffic. Only celebrities and large companies get that.

You may be wondering how online media sites are making millions on advertising. For a media site to have an office in Manhattan or San Francisco with a staff of ten, they need perhaps a million dollars in annual revenues, which means about $80,000 per month. To earn that with digital ads, they need 12.5 million monthly unique visitors, which would make them bigger than *TIME* magazine or HP (to see the traffic of websites, see quantcast.com/top-sites).

When you ask media sites about the number of unique monthly visitors or RPM, they won't tell you. Why? The numbers are bad. Their RPMs are lower than mine because large publishers get bulk RPMs, which are lower. I doubt many of those sites can even pay the rent.

What about video? YouTube's RPM is $2.07. If your cat is a YouTube superstar and gets a million views, you only get $2,070.

So how are these sites making money? They're not. They're using the investors' money to cover salary, costs, and rent to grow big enough to sell the site to a large company. They'll make money by selling the site, not in advertising. How will the large company make money? Well, that'll be someone else's problem, won't it?

Why are these numbers so low? Don't people make big bucks with blogs? Back in 2005, I got 60-70,000 monthly visitors and Google also paid a higher RPM, so I got $12,000 per year from Google. But in 2014, there are 175 million websites and six hundred billion pages, so traffic is diluted. People also spend time on social media, apps, movies, and games which also lowers traffic to websites. For the last five years, I've seen a steady drop in traffic.

So what does this mean for your blog? You might get enough to cover the site hosting costs and maybe once a month, you'll be able to buy a hotdog with all the fixings.

The point of your website and blog isn't to make money on those. Just as with books, the goal is to build up credentials to get opportunities.

## How to Track Success?

Let me add a quick section on tracking and metrics. You can use any web analytics package, including Adobe Omniture Site Catalyst, IBM Coremetrics Analytics, or Google Analytics. They do pretty much the same thing. For most, Google Analytics is a good solution. It's also free.

Web analytics will track the number of visitors, what sites they come from, and what devices they use (desktop, tablet, cell phone). If you're collecting leads or selling on your site, you can also track that.

But analytics isn't very useful. After you've written several books and spoken at countless events, the cumulative effect of your work that leads to results.

## Summary of this Chapter

You'll finally meet your audience in the months after you've published the book. You'll talk with them at bookstores, speaking events, and trade shows. You'll also meet lots of new friends.

# The Author Speaks: Andreas Ramos

Several people said I should also be interviewed. My cat asked the questions.

I started writing for computer magazines while I was still in college. Publishers saw those articles and asked if I'd write a book. I've written nine books so far on technical stuff. My next few books will be for a wider audience.

## Why Do You Write?

I love to learn about things and I found that if I write about it, I'll understand it better. I also like to share what I've learn.

## How Has Writing Affected Your Life and Career?

My books have given me lots of connections. I've interviewed people and I've met many readers. In the early 90s, I joined the National Writers Union (NWU) and became one of its leaders, where I met thousands of writers. That got me into technical writing in Silicon Valley, which I did for ten years.

## How Did You Find and Choose Your Publisher?

I begin to look for bigger publishers. I found a publisher who didn't have a current title on the topic and I offered to write the book.

## Do You Prefer Self Publishing or Traditional?

That's a very hard question for me. It's great to work with the people in traditional publishing because they really understand what it means to write and produce books. Self publishing works well if you have experience in writing and publishing.

How to Write a Book! by Andreas Ramos

### What's Your Experience with Self Publishing?

The downside of self publishing is the huge amount of non-writing work. I have to create and manage mailing lists, stand in line at the post office to send 45 books, and deal with accounting and taxes.

### What's Your Experience with Traditional Publishing?

Luckily, I've worked with publishers who I trusted and liked, so my experience has been good.

### Do You Have an Agent?

There aren't agents for technical nonfiction books, so I've never had to deal with agents.

### Did a Lawyer Review Your Contract?

At first, I asked lawyer friends to read my contracts, but there wasn't anything to change. After a while, I knew the publishers so well that sometimes, we kinda forgot to use contracts. Once, we signed the contract after the book had already been published!

### What's the Best Way to Promote Your Book?

I've used Google Adwords, Twitter, social media, and so on. I find the best way is my monthly newsletter. I've been sending out a monthly email to my friends for nearly 20 years. Every time I send it out, I get several dozen replies.

### What Would You Have Done Differently?

In the beginning, I'd let two or three years go by between books. I didn't realize how important it was to write more books. I didn't see how to use books as part of my career. I should have written a book every year.

# 16. In Closing: Start Writing!

## The Point of All This

We started with a clear goal. Remember this book's title? *Write a book to get more opportunities*.

To do that, we looked at the process of writing books. But as we got into the details, it became hard to remember what the point was.

And you've seen by now, non-fiction books don't make much money. But that's not the goal.

Books are a great way to build credibility, authority, and trust. As you research, you'll learn your field. When you interview people, you'll meet them and many others. You'll get requests to speak at conferences and events. You'll write what you know and others will see you as an expert.

You'll write books to get projects, contracts, job offers, and business proposals. To improve your career. To do well.

When I told my friends I was writing a book on how to write a book to further your career, they said, "*OMG! I need that book!*"

So that's who I wrote this book for. I wrote it for you.


Andreas Ramos,
Palo Alto, August 18th, 2014

# 17. Resources

## Contact Me

You're welcomed to contact me. Let me know if you have a question. I'll reply. My website is andreas.com and the book's webpage is andreas.com/book-write-a-book.html

## Updates and More Information

For updates and new books, sign up for my newsletter at andreas.com.

## Books about Self Publishing

Several books on self publishing I found to be useful:

- You must get Carla King's *Self-Publishing Boot Camp* (2nd ed., Misadventures Media, 2012) and *How to Self-Publish Your Book* (PBS MediaShift, 2013). She has written a number of books about her motorcycle travels, which she self published. Based on her experience, she teaches courses on self publishing. Her book was my roadmap for my last two books. Go to SelfPubBootCamp.com.

- Mark Coker of Smashwords.com has lots of useful information on self publishing, such as the Smashwords FAQ.

- Guy Kawasaki's *APE: How to Publish a Book* (Nononia Press, 2012) has tips based on his experience in self publishing.

- *The Writer's Market*, by Robert Brewer (93rd ed., Writer's Digest Books, 2013) lists thousands of publishers and what they publish. Updated yearly. Available at most libraries.

## My Other Books

You can find useful stuff in my other books:

- Learn more about SEO with the *SEO eBook*. How search engines index, evaluate and rank sites. Free at andreas.com.

- Learn how to set up and use Google Adwords. Read chapter 6 of *Search Engine Marketing* (McGraw-Hill, 2009).

- Learn about content marketing and how to use it with *The Big Book of Content Marketing* (Andreas.com, 2013). At andreas.com.

- Learn how to calculate key performance indicators (KPI), cost-per-lead (CPL) and cost-per-acquisition (CPA). Get my *KPI eBook* free at andreas.com

- Learn how to use Twitter. Read #*TwitterBook* (Andreas.com, 2013).

Visit andreas.com to find where to get these books.

## How to Find Copyeditors

The following copyeditors edited this book: Gillian Bagwell (team leader) (GillianBagwell@hotmail.com), Isabelle Pouliot (Isabelle@desiu.ca), Jennifer Skancke (jen.skancke@gmail.com), Sean Morales (SeanFMorales@gmail.com), Steven Nelson (SroyNelson@gmail.com)

## Files on the Book's Webpage

The following checklists, contracts, and files are at my andreas.com website:

- Checklist for indexing
- Checklist for producing the print version
- Checklist for releasing your book
- Contract for contractors
- Contract for model release

- Contract for your copyeditor

- Interviews with authors and publishers

- Copy of the cover for this book (front, spine, back)

- And more. See the webpage.

## List of Clickable Links In the book

Here are the links in this book. You can also find a clickable list at this book's webpage:

- Find copyeditors at EditorsForum.org, Editcetera.com, The-EFA.org

- Grammar and punctuation at ThePunctuationGuide.com

- Learn how to self publish at SelfPubBootCamp.com

- See the amount of traffic at top websites at Quantcast.com/top-sites

- Question-and-answer sites at Answers.yahoo.com, AllExperts, theanswerbank.co.uk, Quora.com

- Find related hashtags at Hashtagify.me

- See traffic for hashtags at Topsy.com

- Scrub an email list at DataValidation.com

- Get crowd funding your book project at Kickstarter, Indiegogo, Pubslush, Inkshare.com, Unbound.com (UK)

- Produce and distribute digital or print books with Amazon.com, Smashwords.com, or Lulu.com

- Cloud storage and file sharing with Box.com, Dropbox, Google Drive, Microsoft OneDrive

- Find free images at commons.wikimedia.org

- Get speaking opportunities at NSASpeaker.org

- Search for copies of your images at TinEye.com

- Find ghostwriters at BlogDash, Blogmutt, Business2Blogger.com, Contently, Docstoc.com, eCopyWriters, Zerys, The 90MinuteBook.com

- Find cover designers and illustrators at eLance.com, ODesk.com, FreeLancer.com

- Keyboards at DasKeyboard.com

- Flesch-Kincaid reading score at readability-score.com

- Voice recognition at Nuance.com

- Ghostwriting Julian Assange's autobiography at http://goo.gl/71P29m

- Repetitive Stress Injury (RSI) at http://goo.gl/CrAKYv

- Mark Coker at Smashwords discusses sales data for thousands of books to show the best price at http://goo.gl/clwxHB

- Study by Dr. Weinberg at Queens College (NYC) on writer income at http://goo.gl/zCgwNw

- McKinsey study shows email is forty times more effective than social media at http://goo.gl/BU28Fv

- FTC Guidelines on Testimonials and Endorsements at http://1.usa.gov/13U7Uin

# 18. Glossary

- **90/9/1 Rule**: In any social community (such as writing, music, medicine, sports, etc.), there are three kinds of participants: the creators who create new ideas, the commenters who talk about those ideas, and the audience.

- **Acquisitions Editor**: The acquisitions editor acquires the books for the publishing house. He knows the market, looks for new writers, and works with previously-published writers. He reads book proposals, selects manuscripts to be printed, and turns them over to the project manager.

- **Advance Reading Copy (ARC):** The ARC is a draft of the book that you share with your subject matter experts and other reviewers.

- **ARC:** See Advance Reading Copy.

- **Audience**: 90% of the people in your community are your audience. The audience follows both creators and commenters. They buy and read books. They also share your books with their friends. Encourage your audience to comment, rate, vote, review, distribute, and share your book.

- **Author**: The author of nonfictions books is an expert on the subject with several years of experience and a working knowledge of the field.

- **Brand Editor**: The brand editors ensures the text and illustrations comply with the company's brand guidelines.

- **Commenters**: 9% of a community is comprised of commenters. The commenters discuss the work of the creative 1%: they're critics, reviewers, editorialists, pundits, bloggers, and so on. They could be staff of a publication or self-appointed with a blog or in an online forum. Encourage critics to comment on your books, but they're not your audience.

- **Copyeditor**: The copyeditor checks voice, clarity, spelling, grammar, punctuation, capitalization, list numbering, illustration labeling, subject-verb agreement, and consistency. She also removes wordiness, triteness, convoluted text, and inappropriate jargon. She checks the content against the style manual. Copyeditors are critical for producing quality. Copyeditor is written as one word.

- **Creators**: 1% of a community is creators. Creators create new ideas, set the agenda, and lead the field. They're also known as the influencers. Your goal is to become a creator in your field. You do this by creating authoritative content, offering leadership by advocacy, and setting an agenda.

- **Developmental Editor**: The developmental editor plans the organization of the content, selects categories and formats, edits headings and outlines, rewrites, restructures content, deletes content to improve flow, and identifies gaps in content. He should be familiar with your field.

- **Independent Publisher**: These are small specialized publishing houses. They may specialize in genre fiction (such as detective or science fiction), business fields, or academic publishing. These are generally led by people who love books. The author writes the book and the independent publisher does the editing, layout, printing, distribution, and marketing. The author gets a royalty.

- **Layout Editor**: The layout editor is an expert with fonts, line spacing, and page layout. She also adjusts headings, footers, and pagination. She turns text into a book.

- **Project Manager (PM)**: The project manager (PM) manages the process of book production. She identifies roles, assigns people, sets up the calendar, supervises deliveries, makes sure everyone is in step, and controls the deadlines.

How to Write a Book! by Andreas Ramos

- **Proofreader**: The proofreader checks the final text against the layout to make sure that all of the changes were made. He also checks pagination, line breaks, and captions.

- **Self-published Author**: The self-published author writes a text and distributes it on his own, either as a digital file or a printed book. The author writes the book and also manages the editing, layout, distribution, and marketing, either by alone or with a team. He produces digital books or printed books. Distribution services may include Kindle, Lulu, Smashwords, Nook, and Amazon. This can also be a PDF by email, posted on a blog or website, or sold at Amazon.

- **SME**: See Subject Matter Experts

- **Subject Matter Experts (SME)**: Subject Matter Experts (SME) have experience and knowledge of your subject. They review the first draft and make suggestions and changes. These can include colleagues and co-workers. You can also add a few non-experts to make sure your book is clear to everyone. You should have about 20 subject matter experts.

- **Traditional Publishers**: Big house publishers take care of editing, layout, printing, distribution, and marketing. The author also gets a royalty.

- **Vanity Press**: A vanity press pretends to be a publisher. You send your manuscript and several thousand dollars and they'll print it for you. These printers take advantage of the author's desperation to be published.

# 19. Index

# More Books by Andreas

## #TwitterBook
### How to Use Twitter
### by Andreas Ramos

Do you "get" Twitter? Finally, a book in plain English about Twitter. What it really is and how to use it. Learn how to use hashtags, get followers, and use Twitter.

Lots of surprising details: What teens are doing on Twitter, how the police use Twitter, and how to use Twitter in a disaster.

- 59 pages, illustrated, index
- ISBN 978-0-9893600-4-3 USA 2013
- See andreas.com

## The Big Book of Content Marketing
### by Andreas Ramos
**amazon** Best Seller

80% of your digital advertising doesn't reach your audience. People delete cookies or use ad blocking software. Use content marketing and people will come to you. Cheaper than ads and it works better.

- Published in the US by Andreas.com and Paris by Betwin Press
- 154 pages, illustrated, index
- ISBN 978-0-9893600-0-5 USA 2013
- See andreas.com

# Silicon Valley Business School

 Opening in 2014, the Silicon Valley Business School (SVBS) will offer a better business school education at a fraction of the price.

Where traditional schools taught students to analyze businesses operated by others, SVBS teaches you how to build your own business. "We're teaching students to be players, not spectators" said David Smith, Dean of the Silicon Valley Business School. "Our graduates will be able to form their own businesses, run their own marketing programs, and negotiate their own transactions."

Courses include patent strategies, contracts, venture capital, mergers, acquisitions, IPO, digital marketing, sales, customer relationship management, finance, and accounting.

SVBS professors and instructors include David Smith, Andreas Ramos, Britten Sessions, Austin Higgins, Dr. J. Moon Kim, Mark Cameron White, and others. Instructors are in the US, Korea, India, Spain, Malaysia, New Zealand, and other countries.

David Osei, founder of Dropify, the Ghanaian startup selected as Grand Prize winner in the prestigious Global Startup Open Competition, comments, "For startups like mine looking to have monumental success like what we see and read about in Silicon Valley, there is no better place to learn best practices than SVBS."

Enrollment is open for courses in Entrepreneurship & Startup Management (svbs.co/16), Digital Marketing (svbs.co/17), Patents & Intellectual Property (svbs.co/22), and Finance/Accounting (svbs.co/23).

Visit SVBS.co or #SVBS.

# Notes